HOW TO DRAW

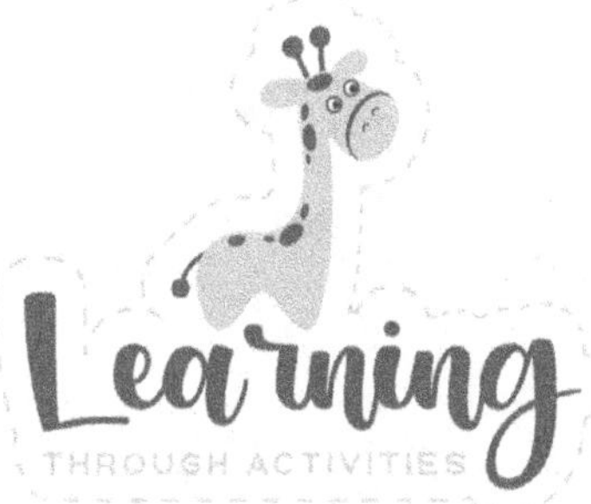

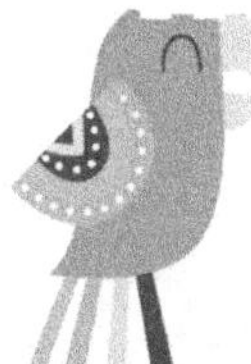

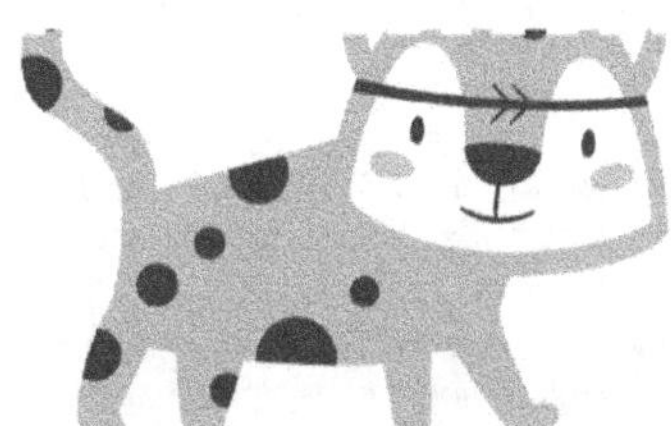

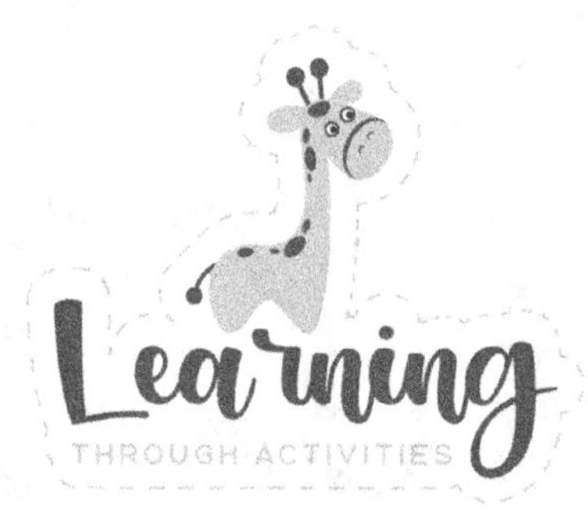

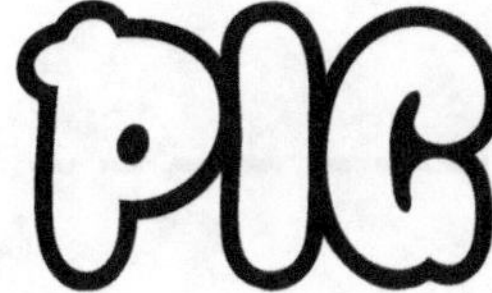 PIG

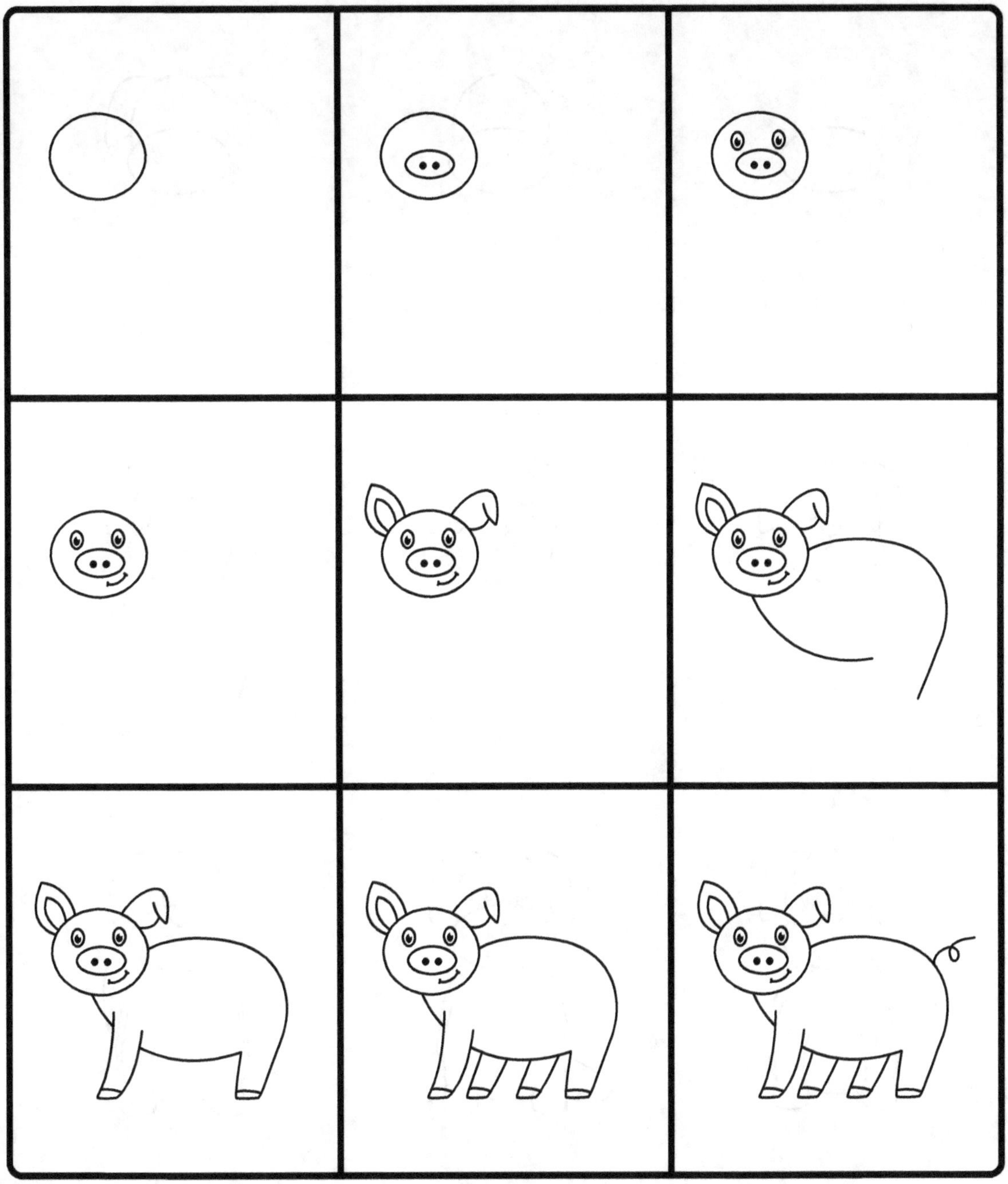

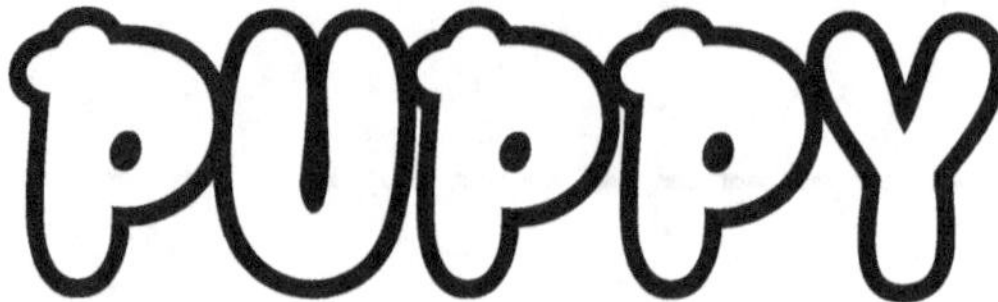

FUN FACT:
DALMATIAN PUPPIES ARE
BORN WITHOUT SPOTS!

BREEDS:
195

JOKE:
WHAT DO YOU CALL A PUPPY
IN THE SUN?
A HOT DOG!

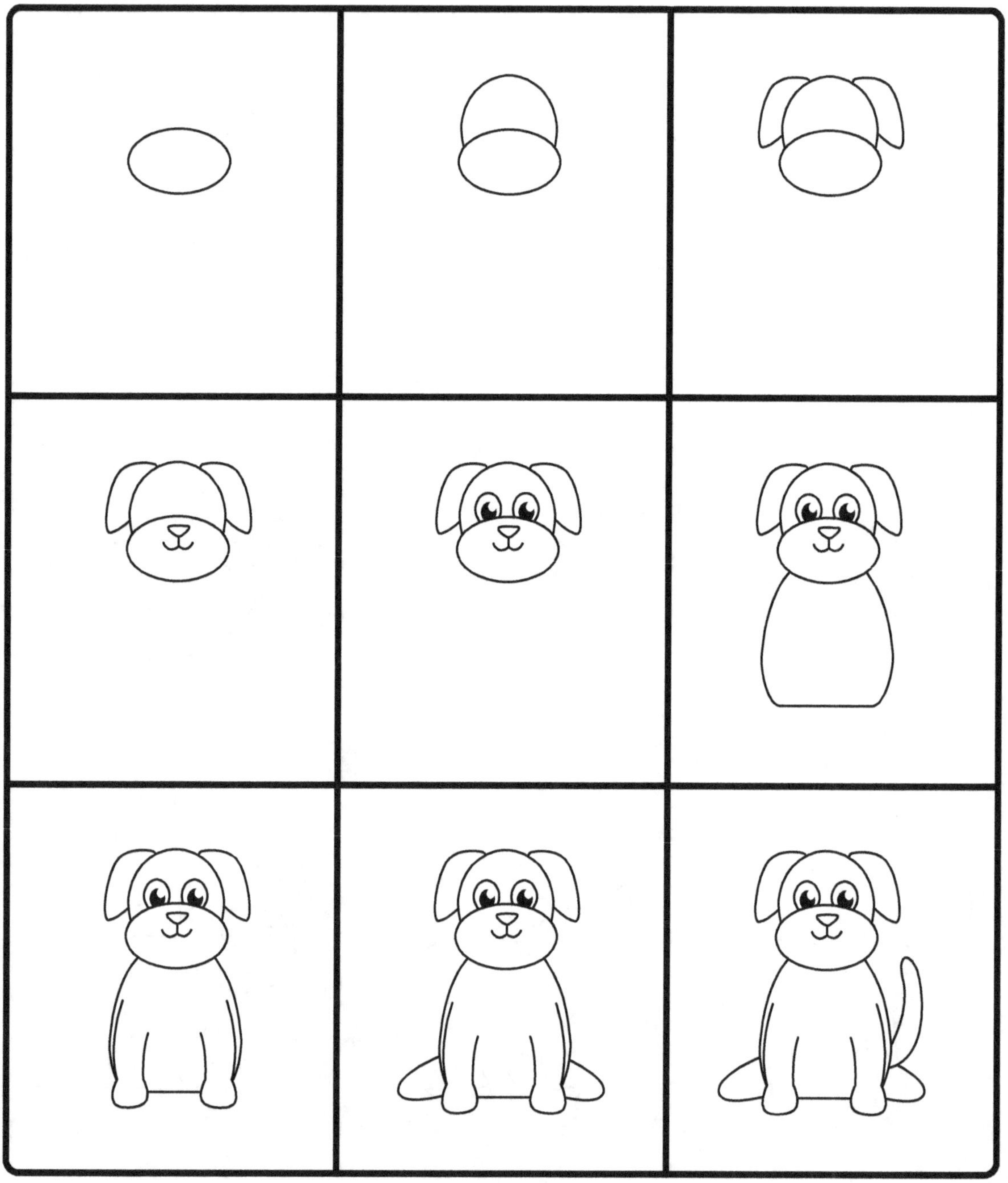

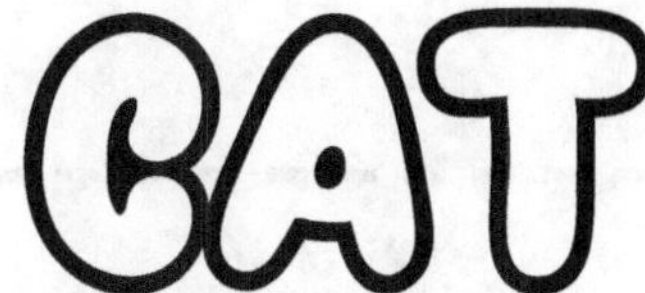

FUN FACT:
CATS ALSO HAVE WHISKERS
ON THE BACK OF THEIR LEGS!

SPECIES:
38

JOKE:
WHAT'S A CAT'S FAVOURITE
COLOR?
PURRRRPLE!

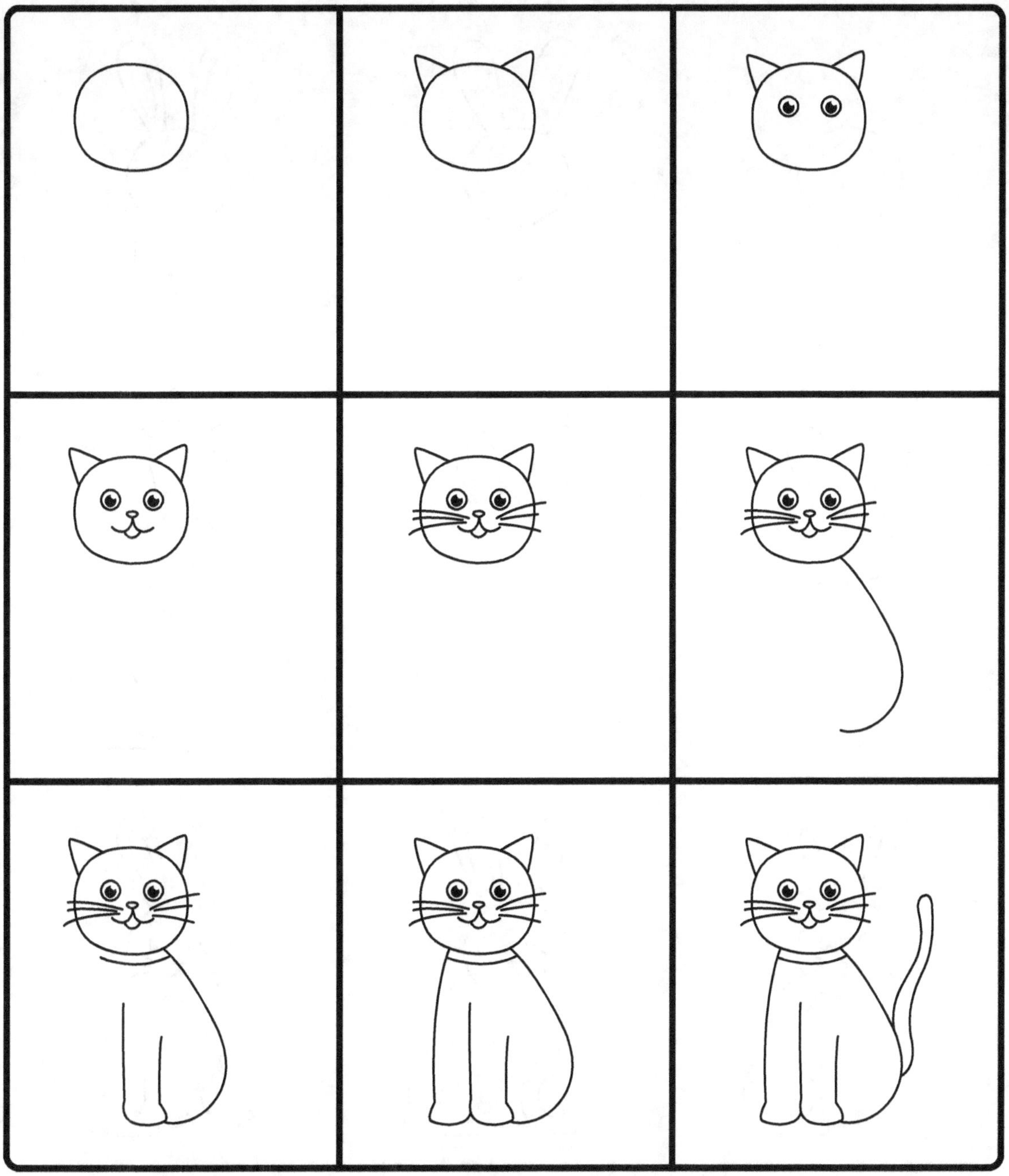

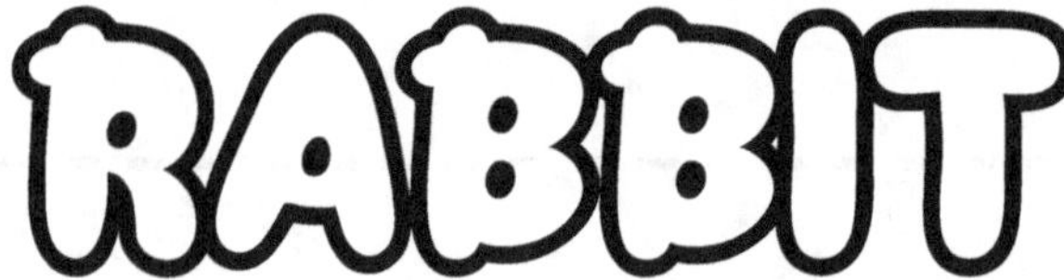 RABBIT

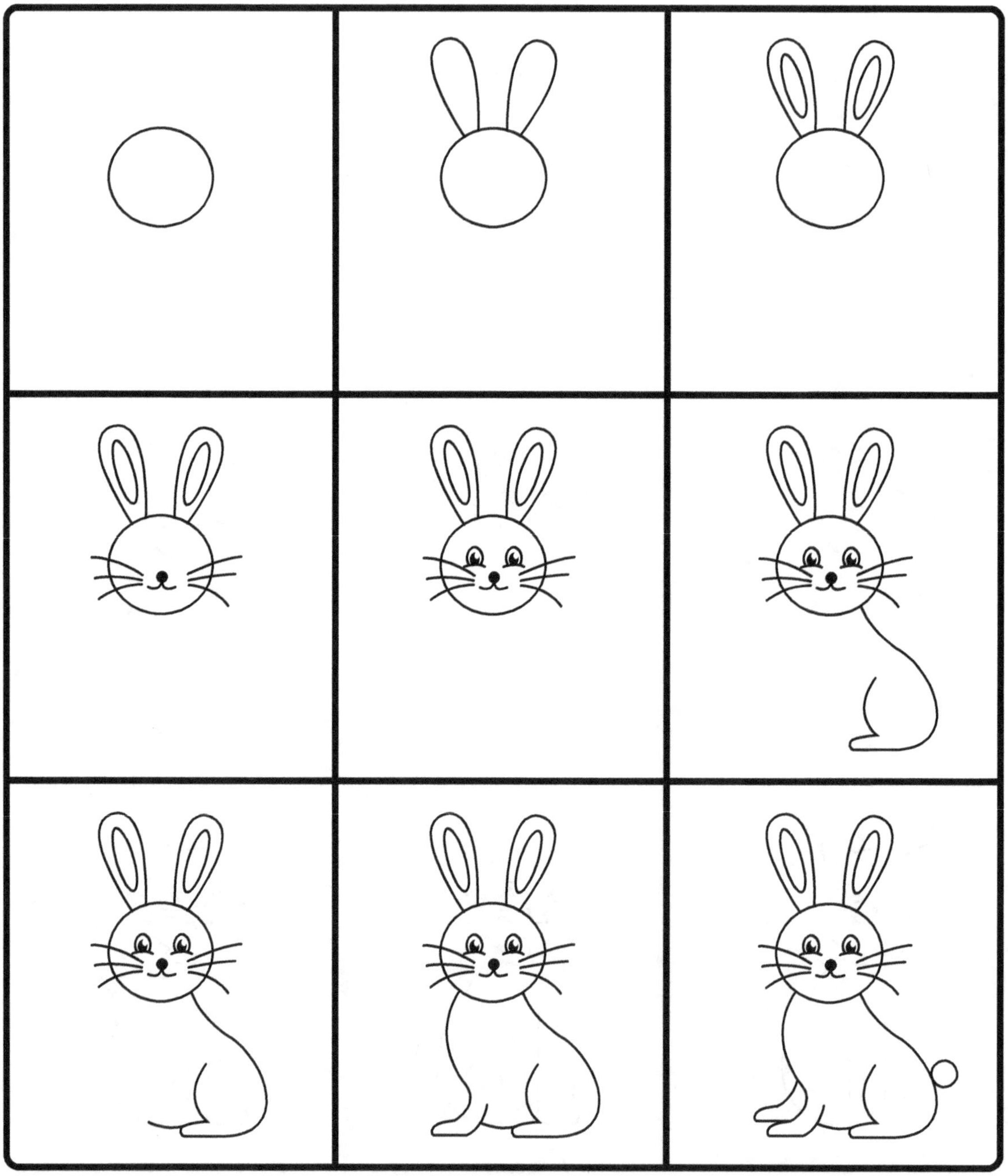

FUN FACT:
RABBITS DO NOT LIKE YOU MESSING UP THEIR AREA AND WILL PUSH THINGS BACK IN PLACE.

SPECIES:
50

JOKE:
WHAT DID THE RABBIT SAY TO THE CARROT?
I LOVE GETTING TO GNAW YOU!

GIRAFFE

FUN FACT:
A GROUP OF GIRAFFES IS CALLED 'TOWERS!'

SPECIES:
4

JOKE:
DO YOU WANT TO HEAR THE JOKE ABOUT THE GIRAFFE'S NECK?
NA, IT'S TOO LONG!

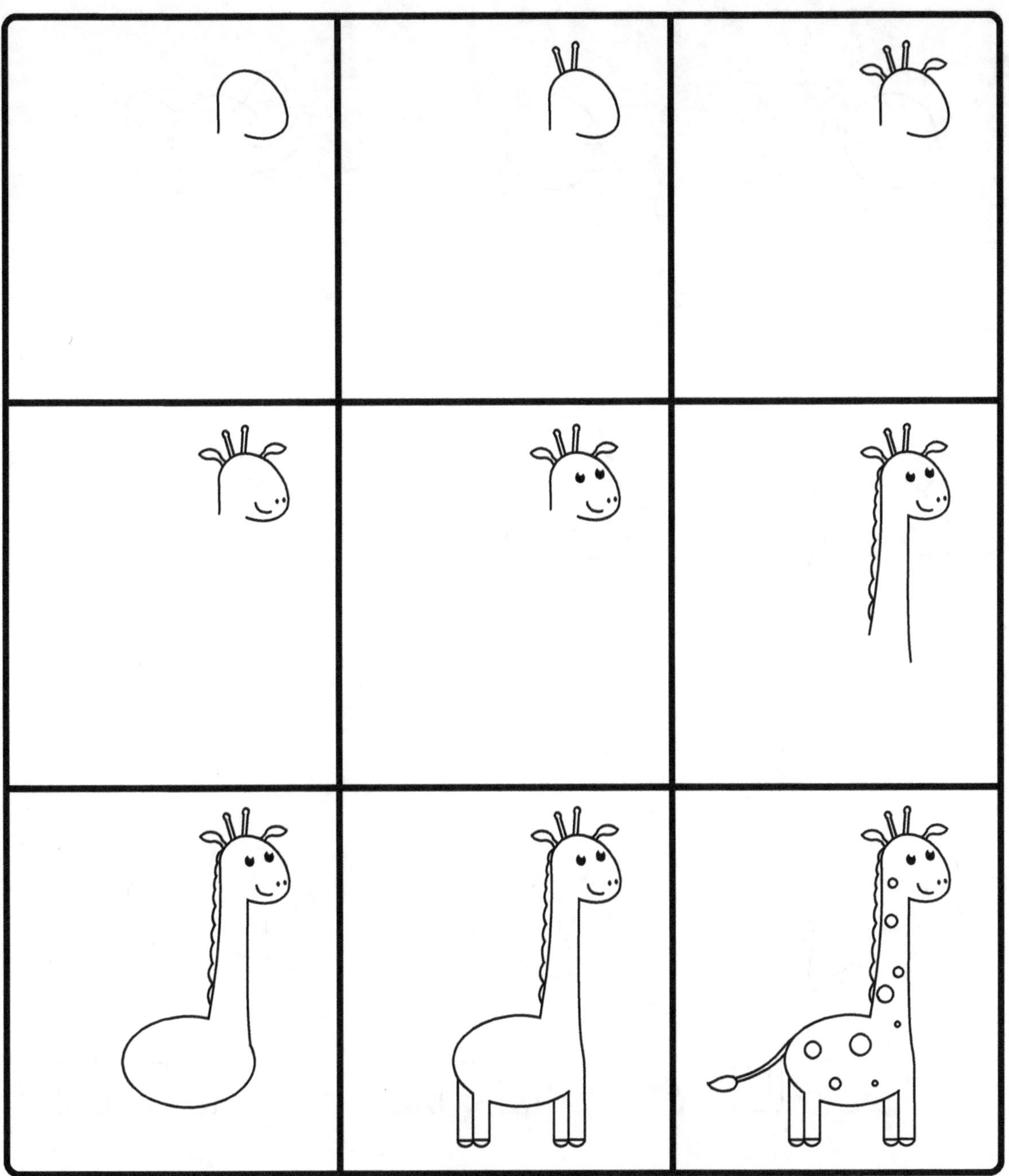

ELEPHANT

FUN FACT:
THEY ARE SUPER EMOTIONAL!

SPECIES:
2

JOKE:
WHAT HAPPENS WHEN AN
ELEPHANT SITS ON YOUR
CLOCK RADIO?
TIME TO GET A NEW CLOCK!

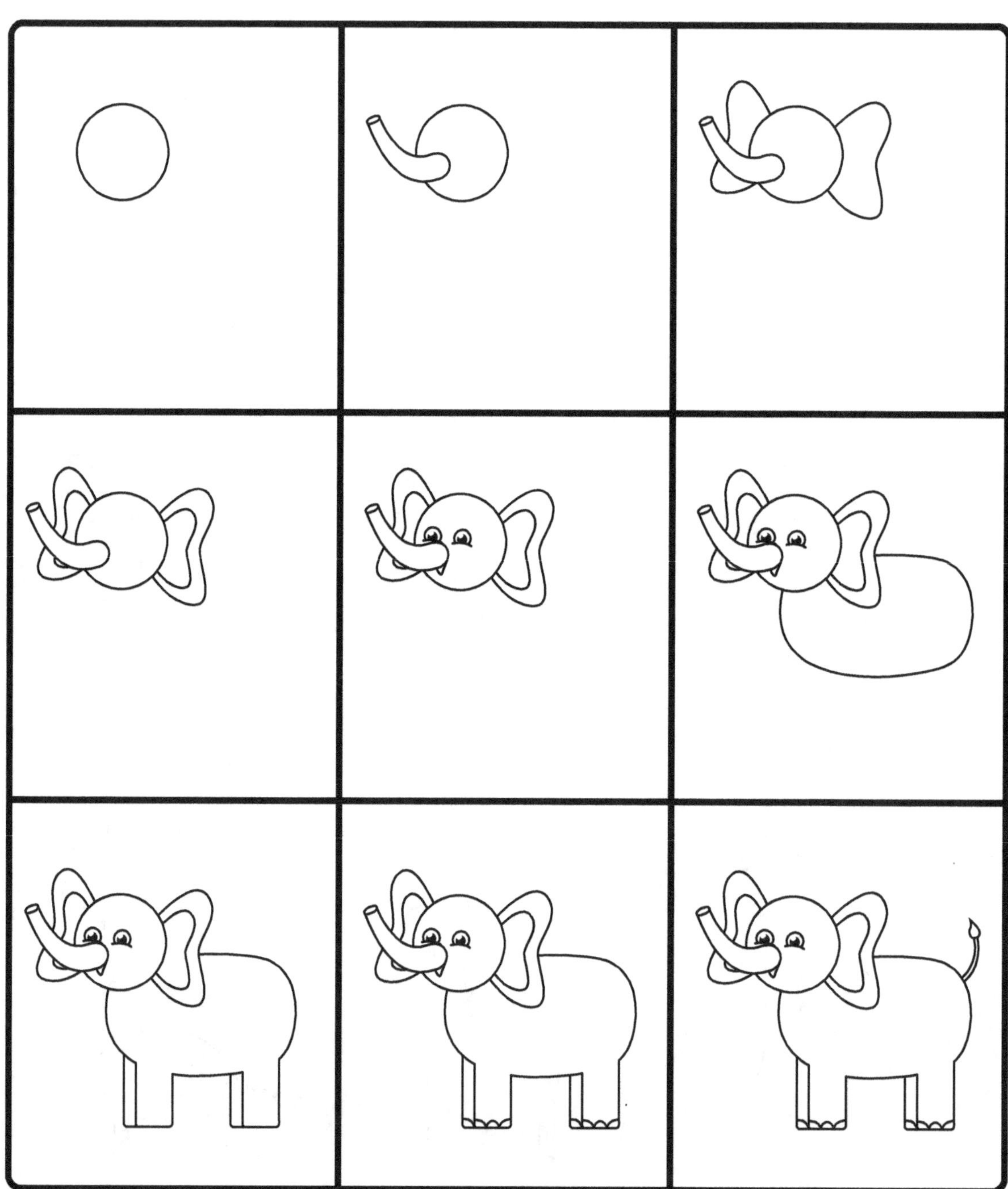

SHEEP

FUN FACT:
SHEEPSKIN IS FIREPROOF.

BREEDS:
200+

JOKE:
WHAT ARE SHEEP'S FAVORITE RESTAURANTS?
ALL YOU CAN BLEAT.

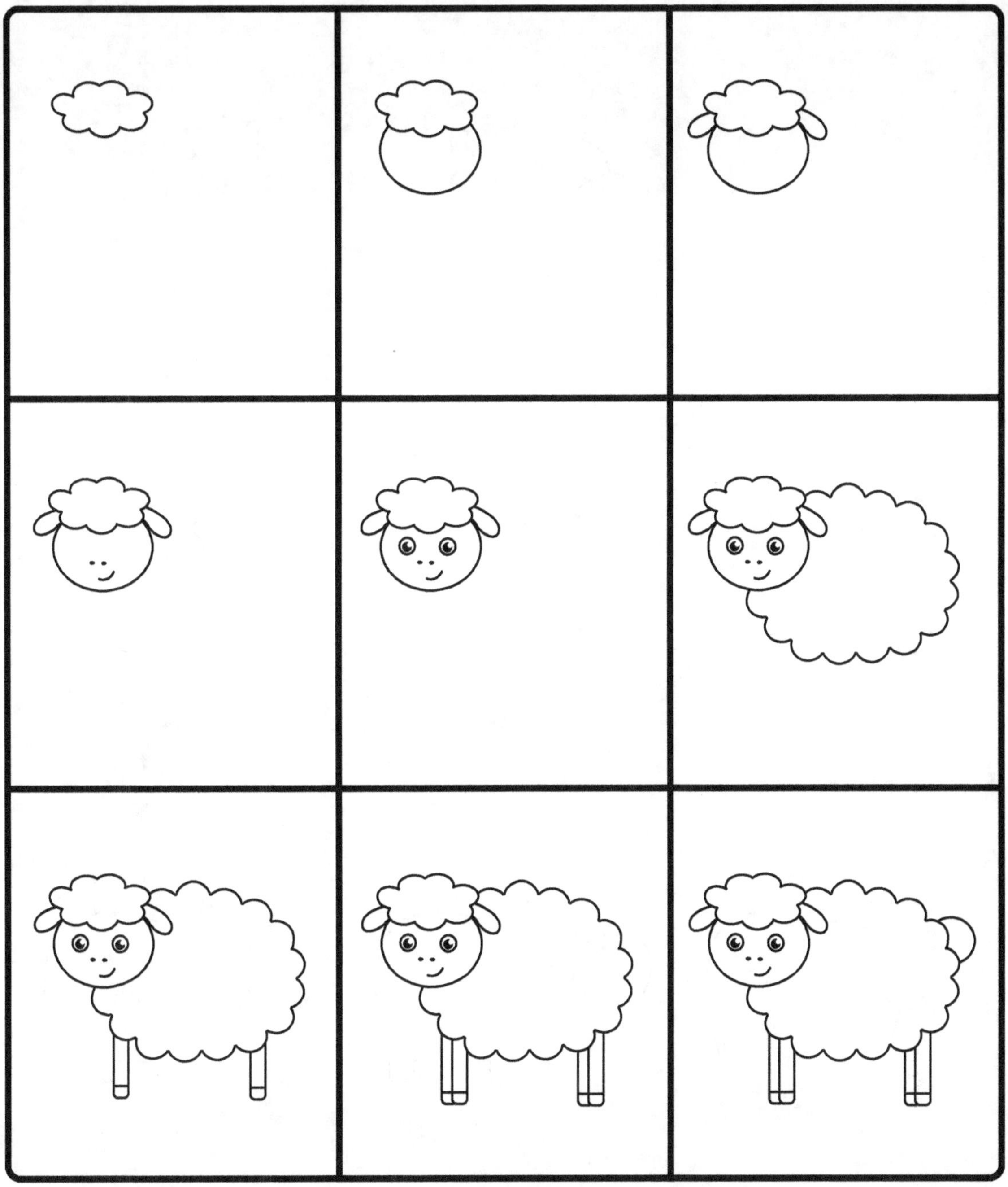

HIPPOPOTAMUS

HIPPOS DON'T ACTUALLY SWIM. THEY SORT OF BOUNCE, WALK AND GALLOP THROUGH THE WATER.

2

WHAT MUSIC DO HIPPOS LIKE BEST?
HIP-HOP.

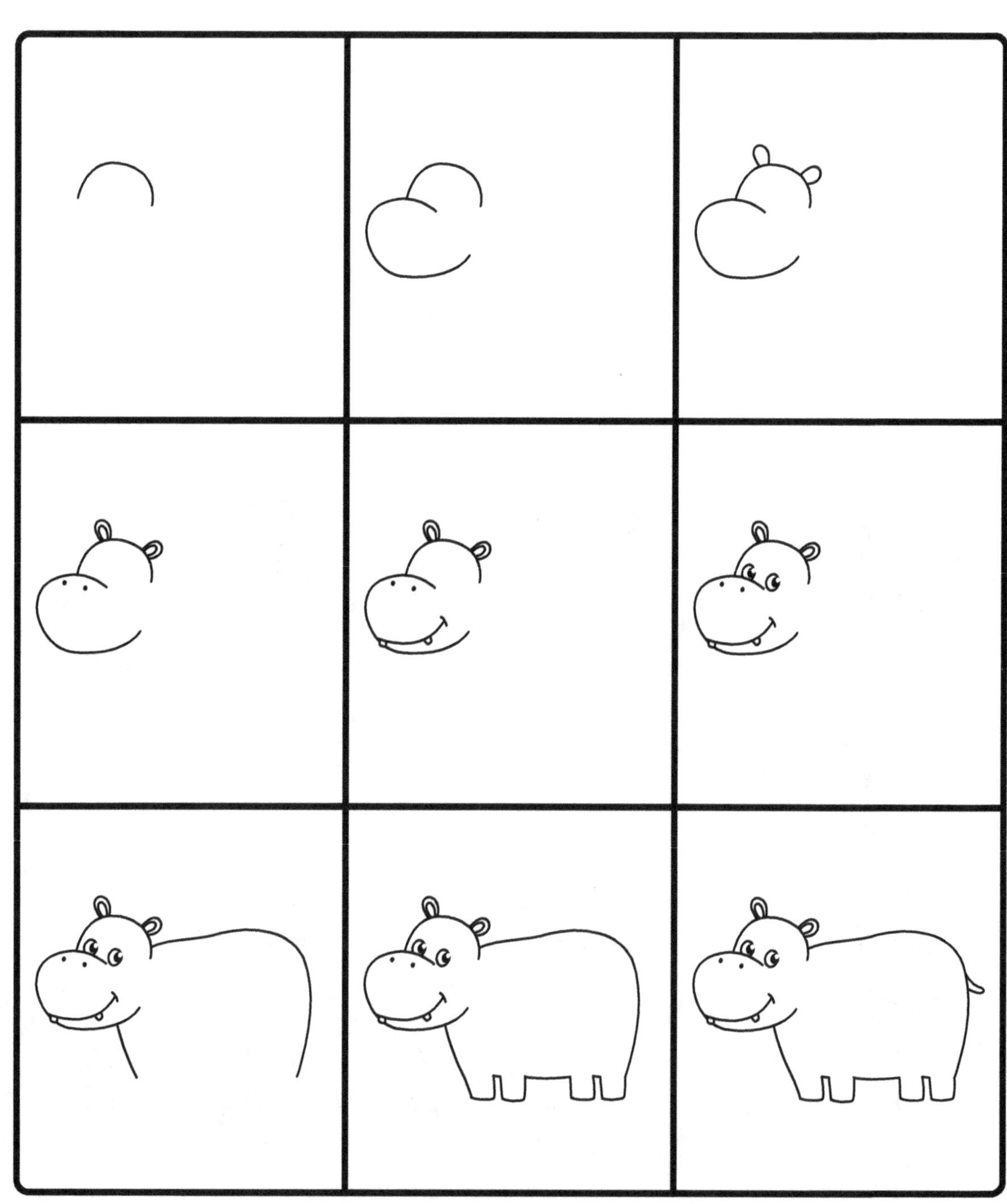

PANDA

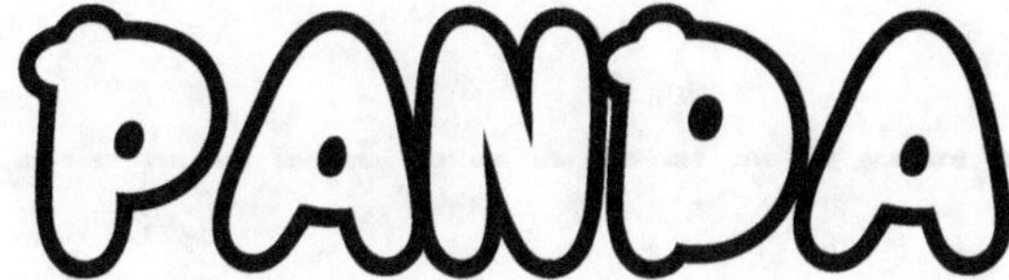

FUN FACT:
GIANT PANDAS CAN SWIM!

SPECIES:
2

JOKE:
WHY DO PANDAS HAVE FURRY
COATS?
BECAUSE THEY'D LOOK SILLY
IN PUFFER JACKETS!

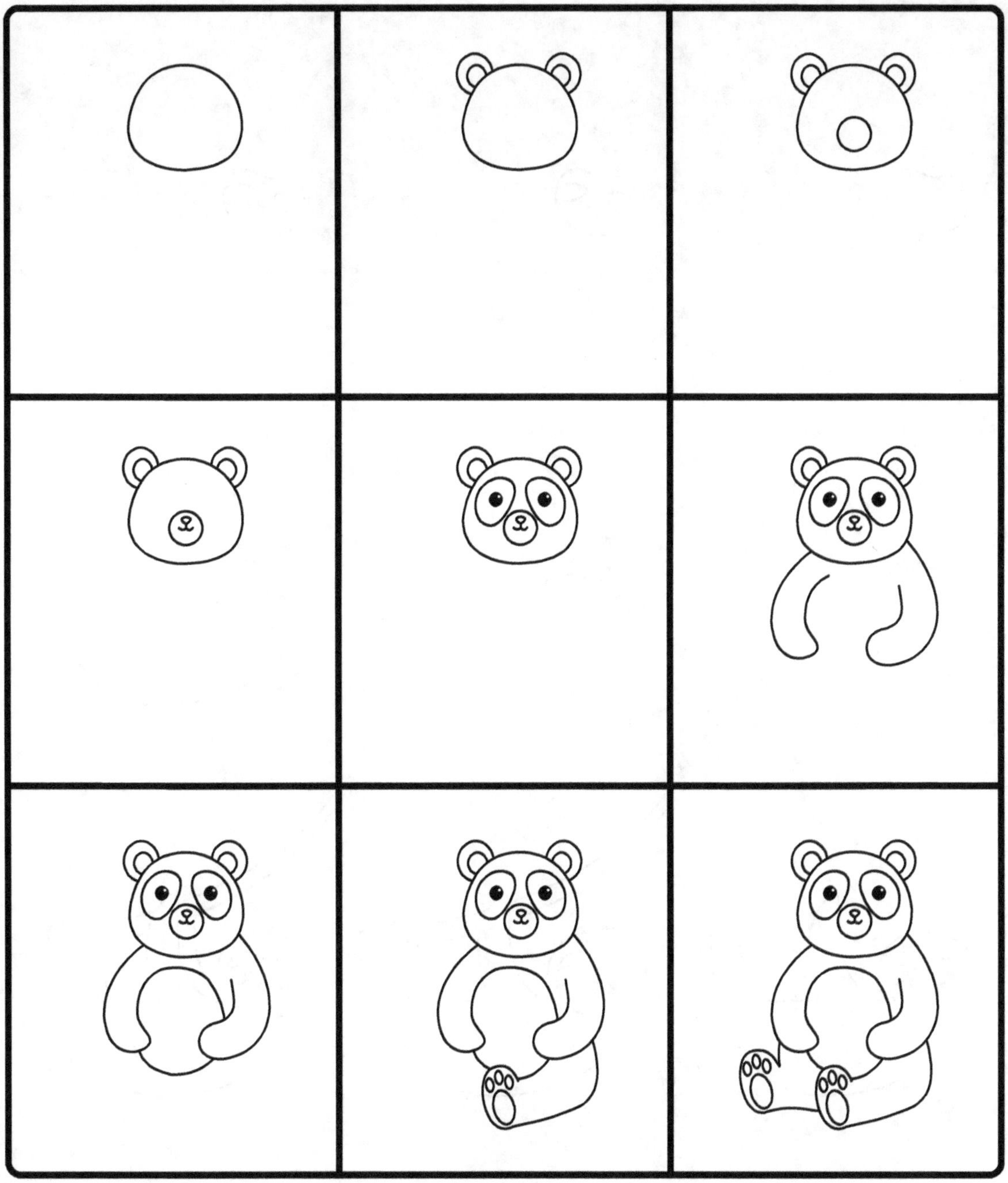

SLOTH

FUN FACT:
THEIR POOS ARE HUGE!

SPECIES:
6

JOKE:
THEY THROW SLOWBALLS.

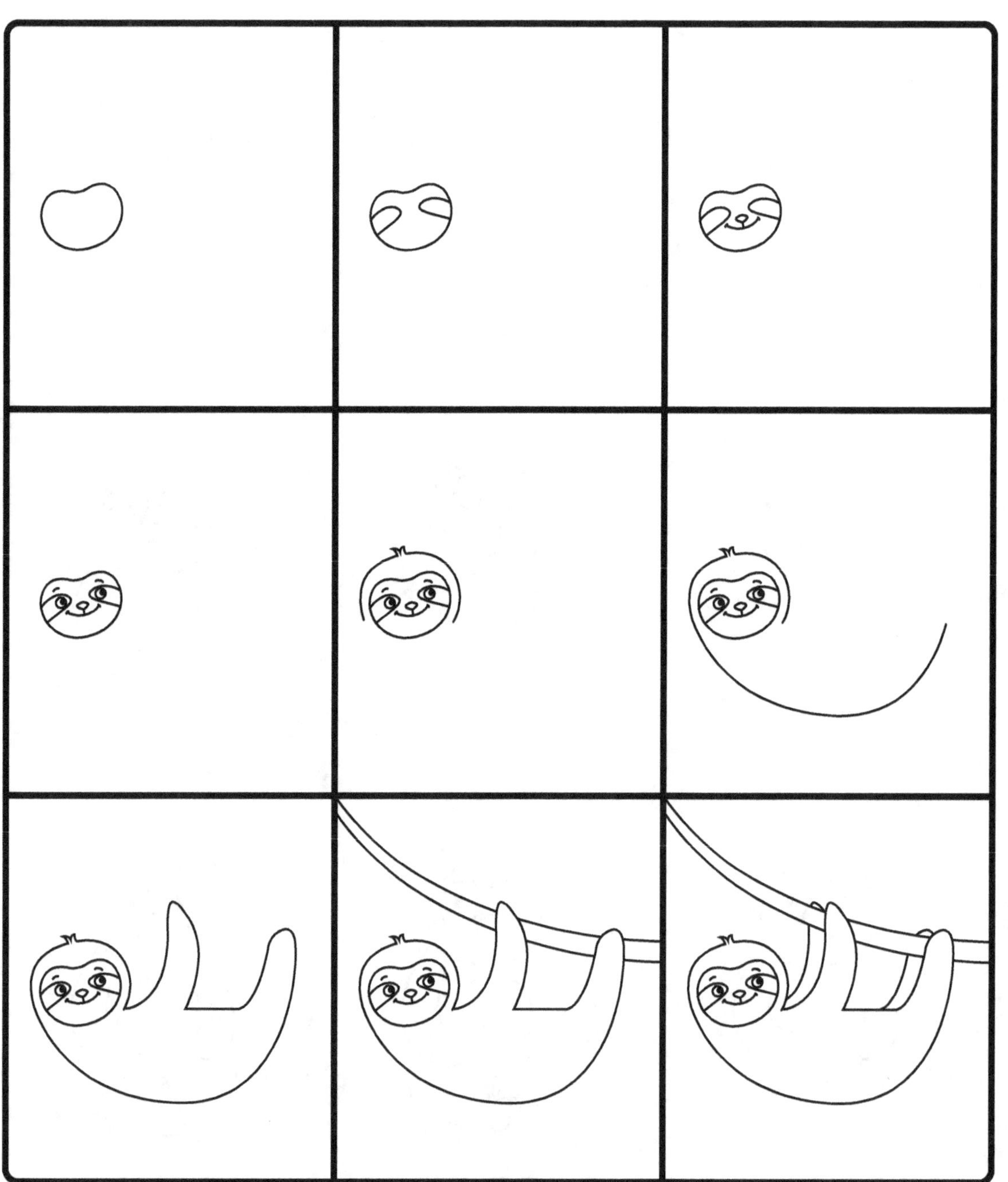

GORILLA

THEY CAN HAVE BABIES WHEN THEY ARE AS YOUNG AS TEN YEARS OLD!

2

HOW DO GORILLAS MAKE GRILLED CHEESE SANDWICHES? UNDER THE GORILLA.

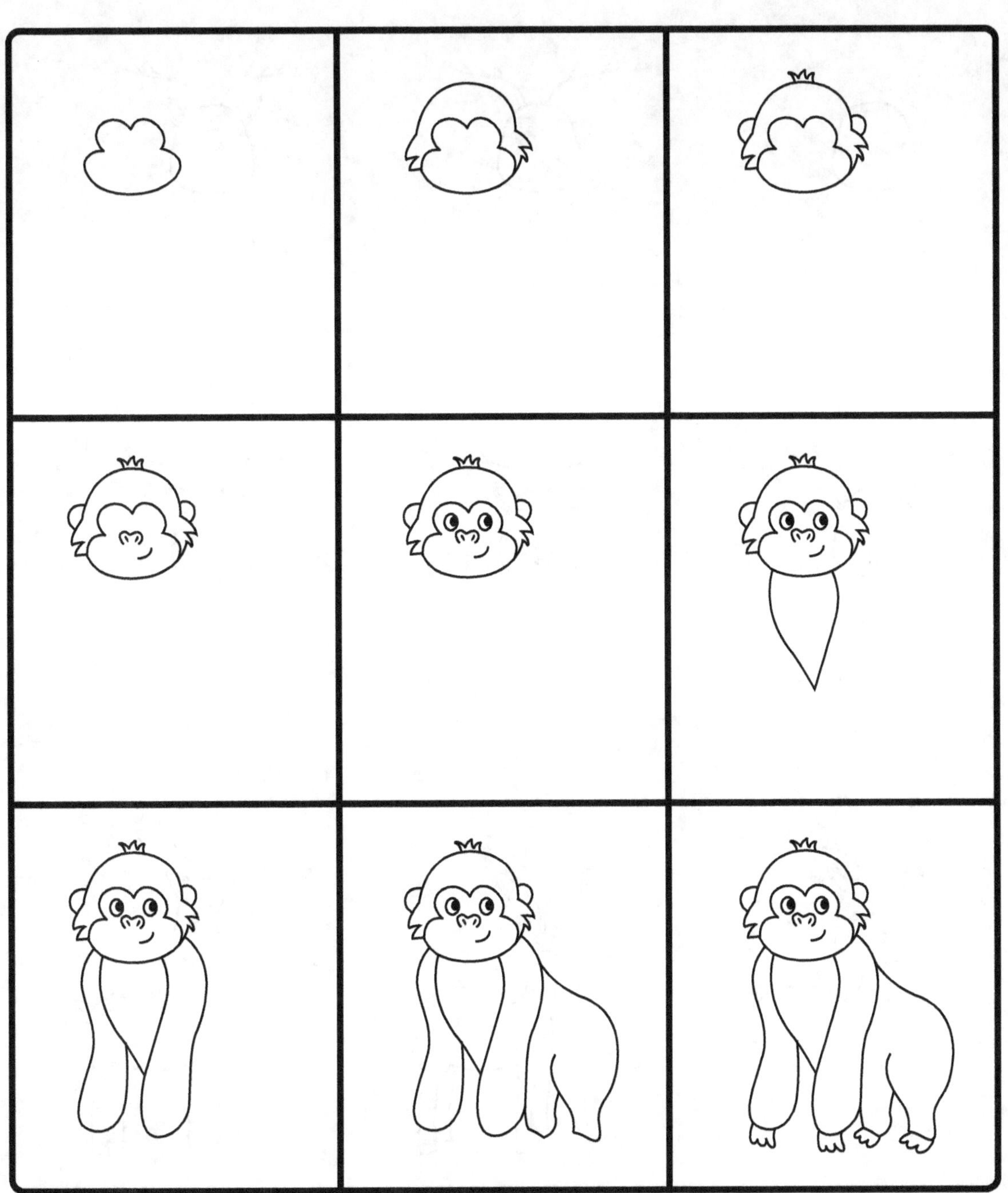

DEER

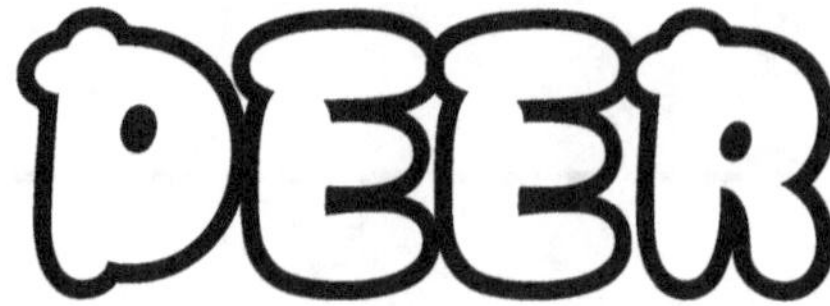

<table>
<tr><td>FUN FACT:</td><td>SPECIES:</td><td>JOKE:</td></tr>
<tr><td>THE LARGEST DEER IS THE MOOSE.</td><td>43</td><td>WHAT DID THE MAN SAY WHEN A DEER RAN IN FRONT OF HIM?
OH, DEER, DEER, DEER!</td></tr>
</table>

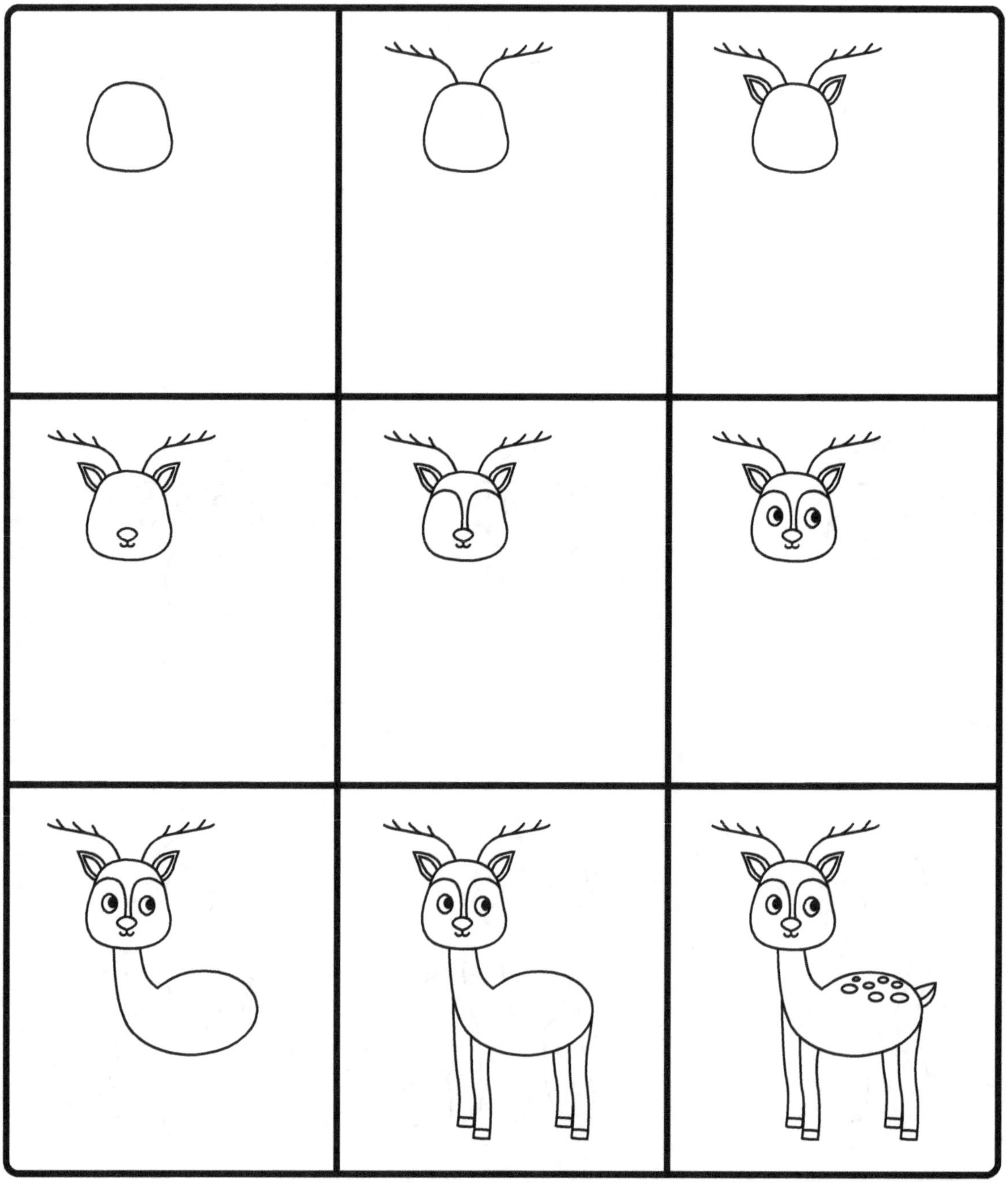

RHINOCEROS

FUN FACT:
A GROUP OF RHINOS IS CALLED A 'CRASH'!

SPECIES:
5

JOKE:
WHAT DO YOU CALL A UNICORN THAT'S GREY, WRINKLY, OLD, AND OVERWEIGHT? A RHINO.

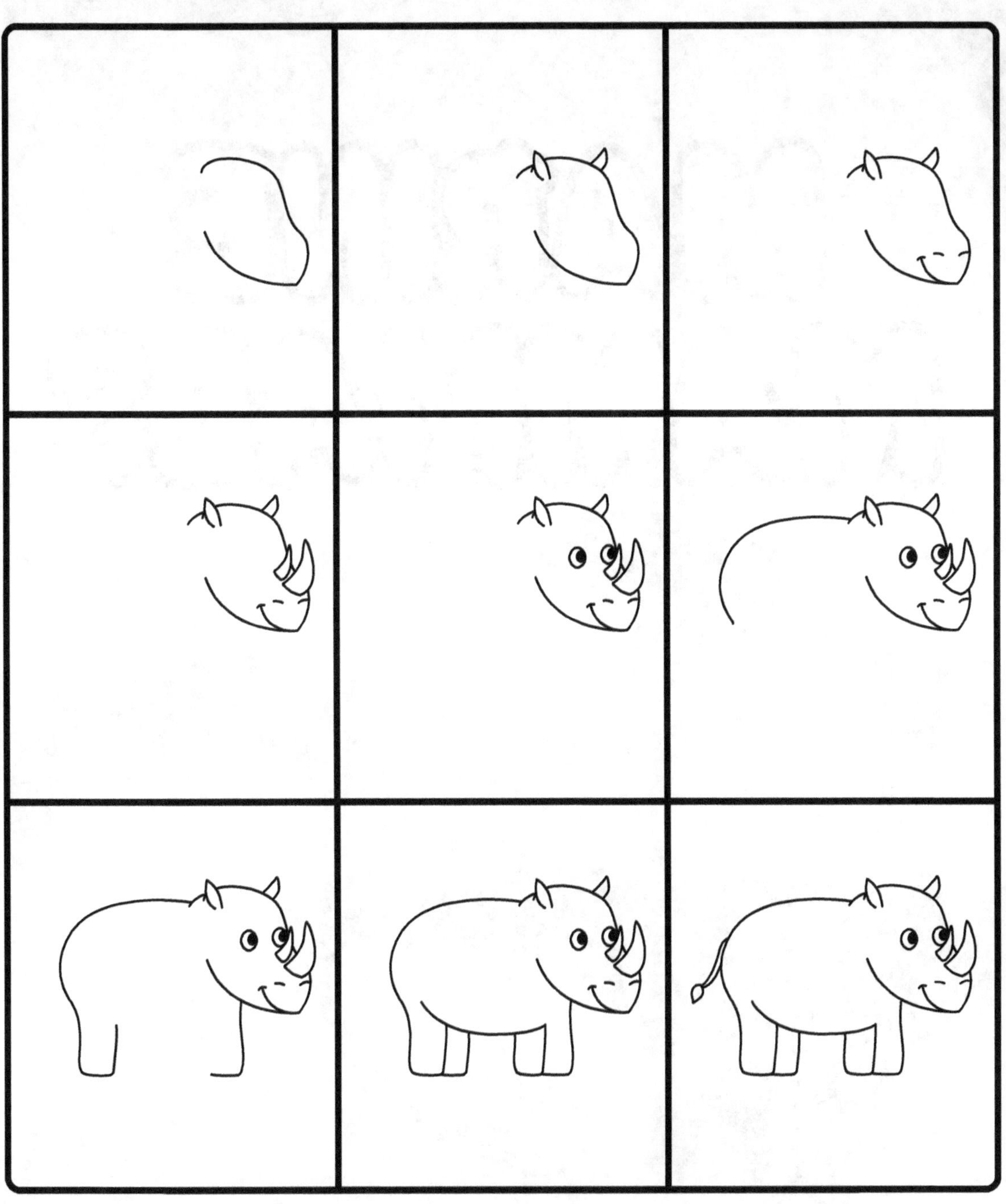

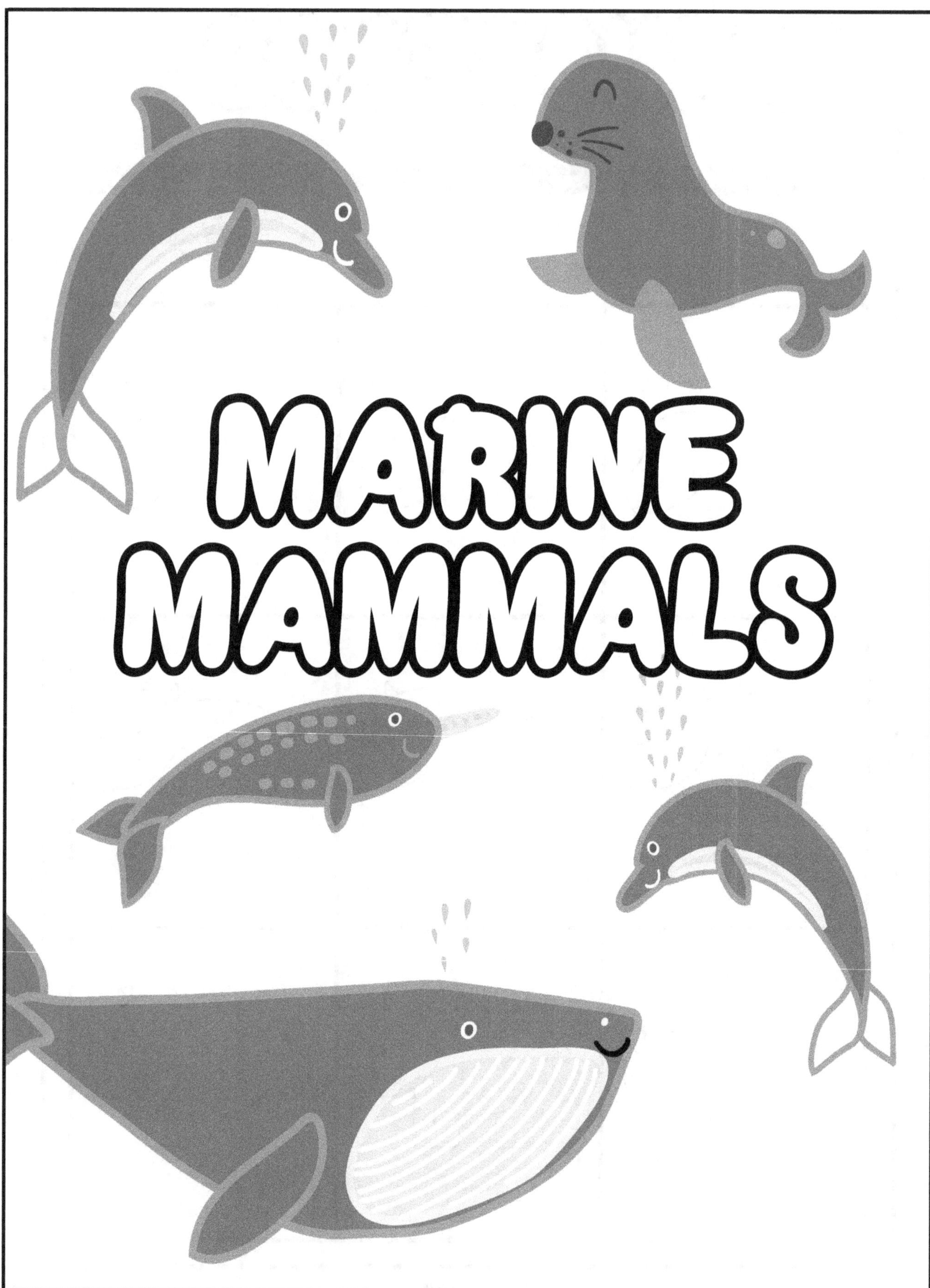
MARINE
MAMMALS

WHALE

FUN FACT:
WHALES ARE VERY LOUD.
THEY CAN BE HEARD FROM
OVER 1000 KM AWAY!

SPECIES:
90

JOKE:
WHAT'S A WHALE'S FAVORITE
FOOD?
FISH AND SHIPS.

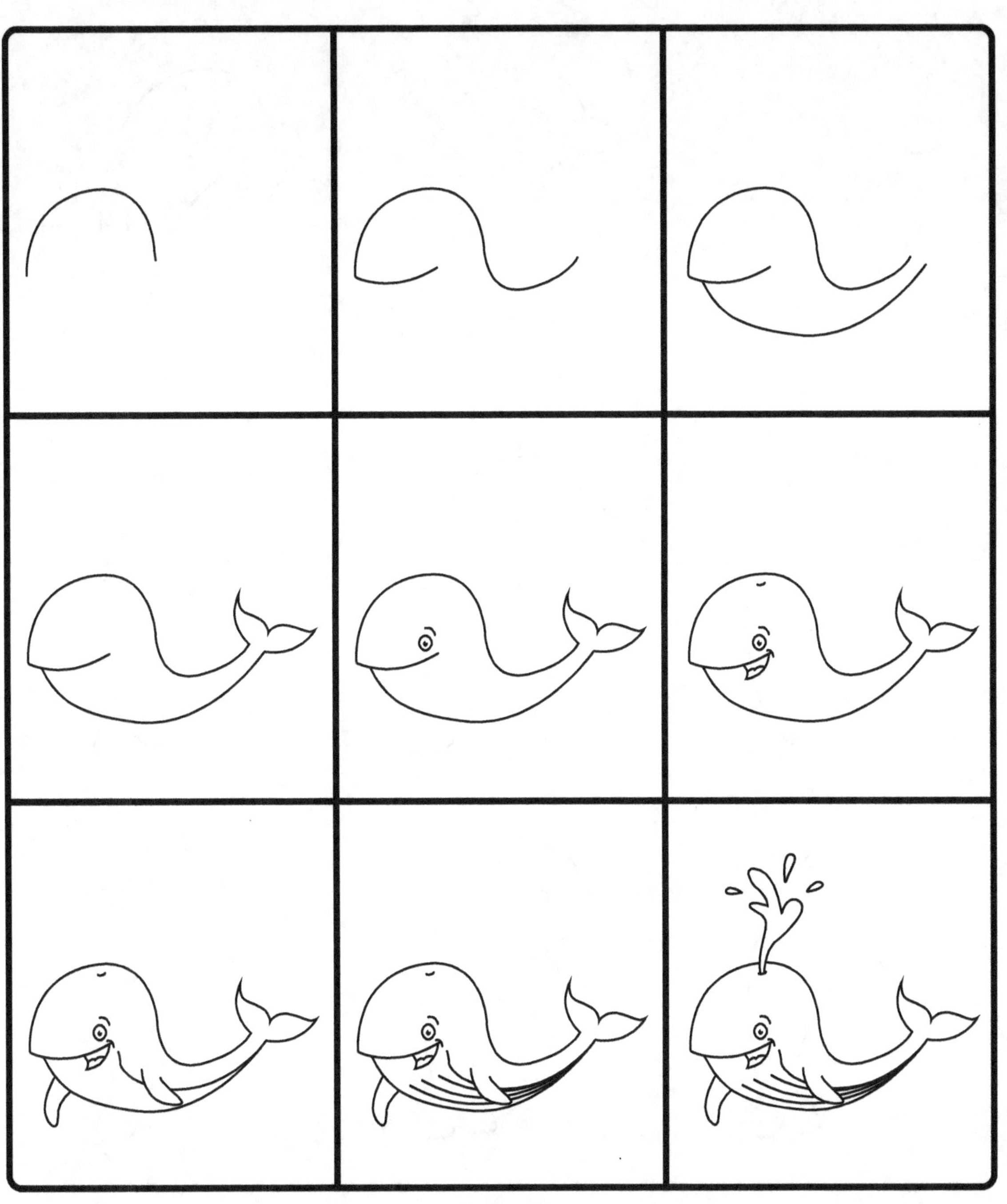

DOLPHIN

FUN FACT:
DOLPHINS GIVE EACH OTHER NAMES - CALLED 'SIGNATURE WHISTLES.'

SPECIES:
49

JOKE:
WHY WAS THE DOLPHIN SAD? HE HAD NO PORPOISE.

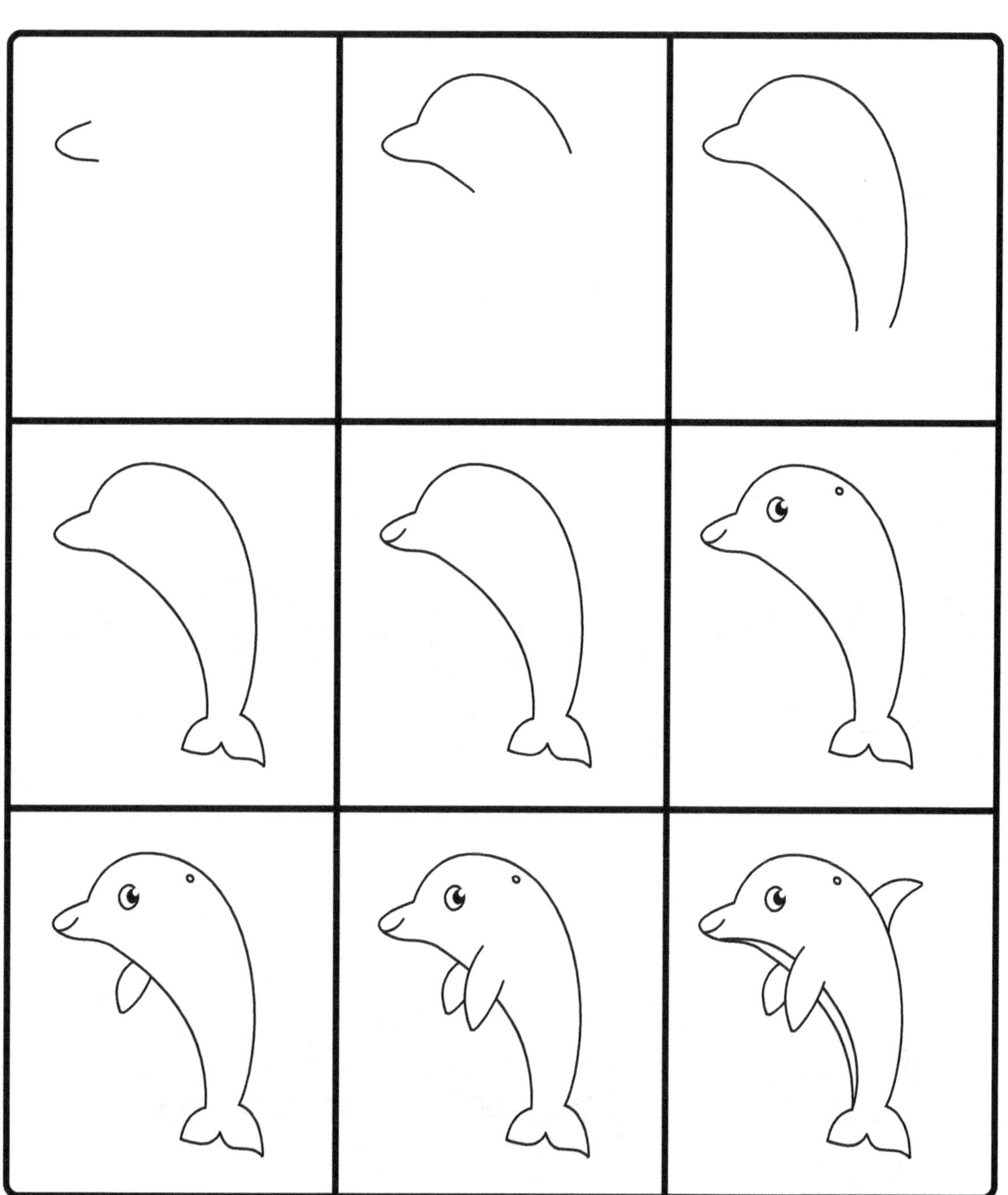

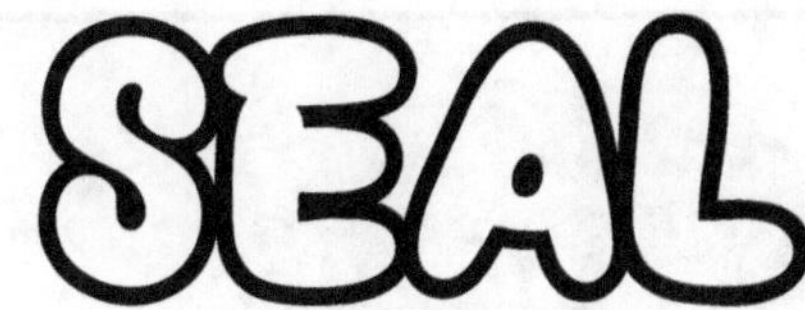 SEAL

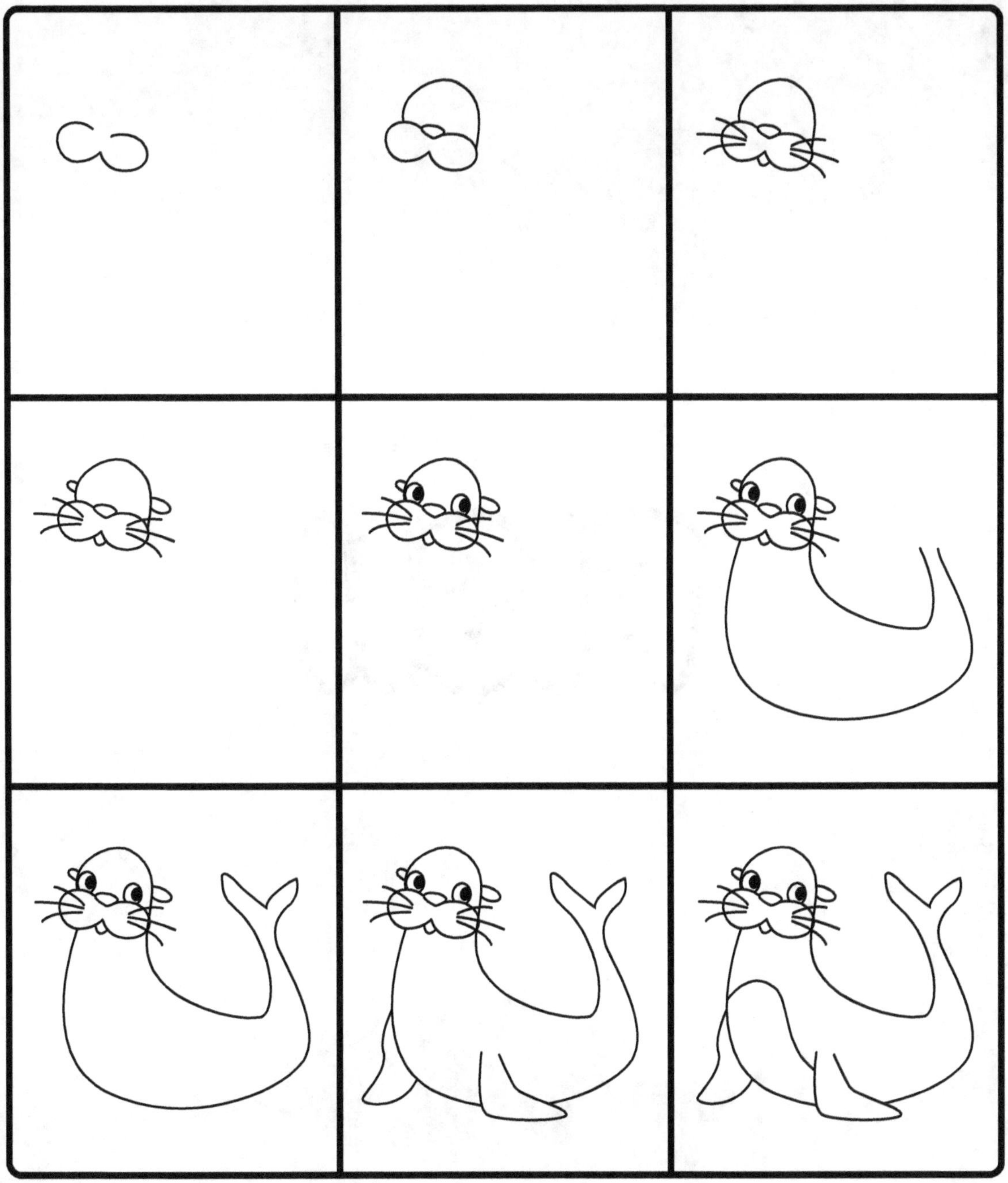

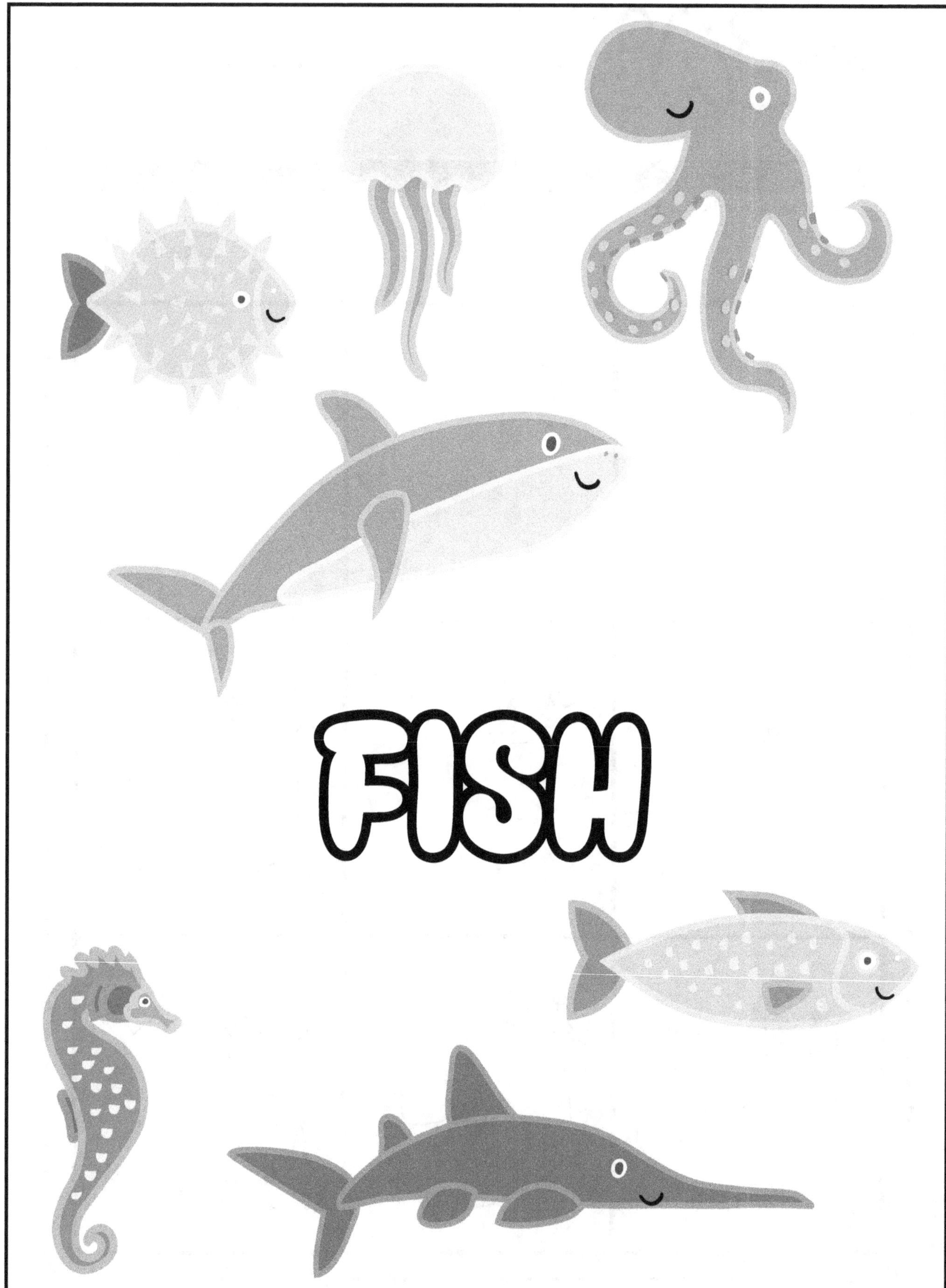

FISH

SHARK

FUN FACT:
SHARKS HAVE BEEN AROUND LONGER THAN TREES.

SPECIES:
400

JOKE:
WHY DO SHARKS PREFER SALTY WATER? BECAUSE PEPPERY WATER MAKES THEM SNEEZE.

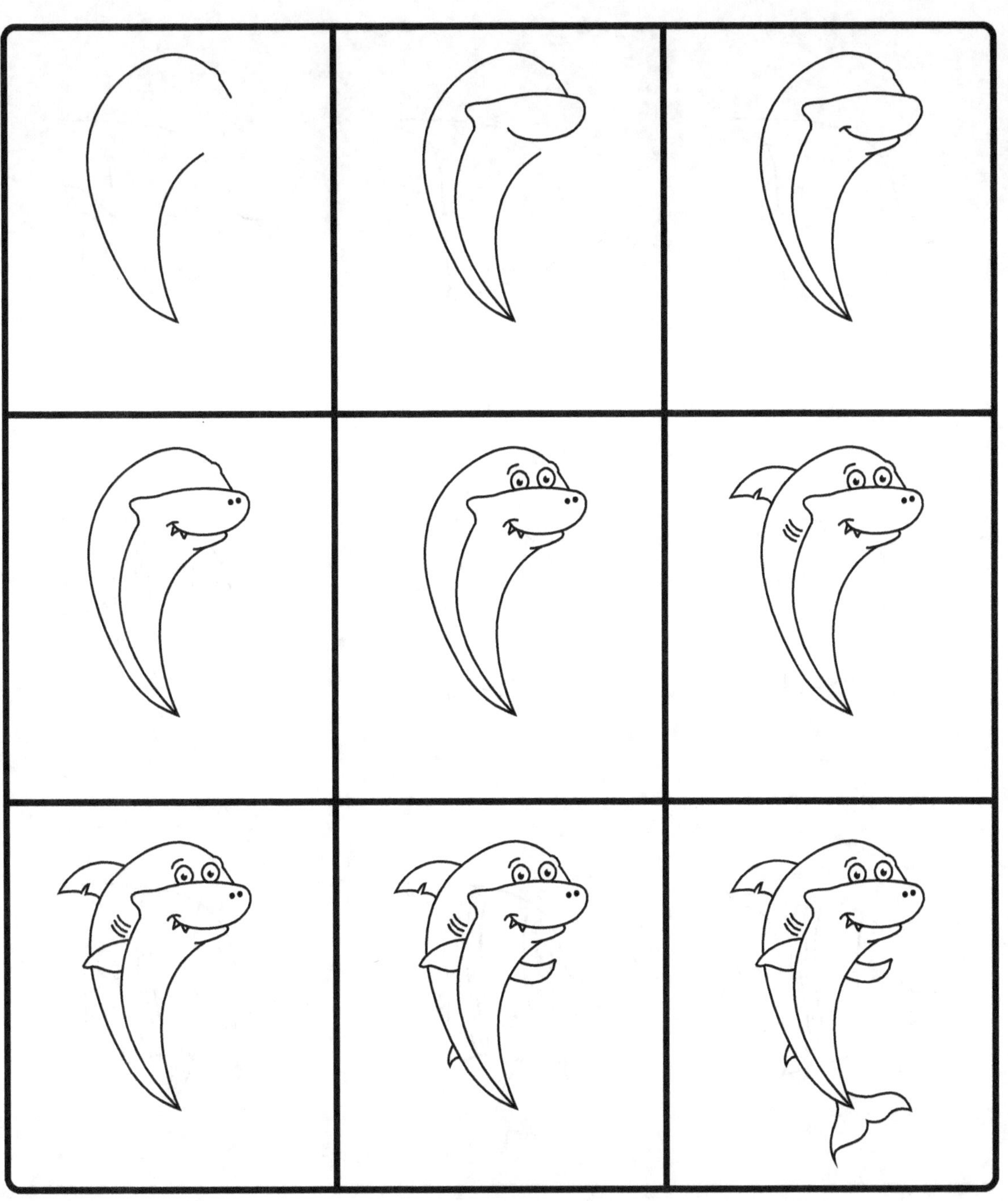

FISH
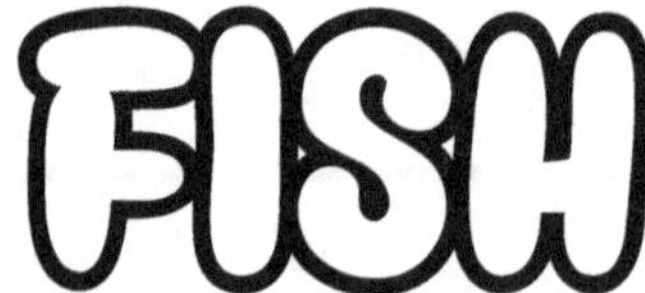

FUN FACT:
HERRING FISH ACTUALLY TALK TO EACH OTHER BY FARTING!

SPECIES:
34,000+

JOKE:
WHAT KIND OF PHONE DO FISH USE?
A SHELL PHONE.

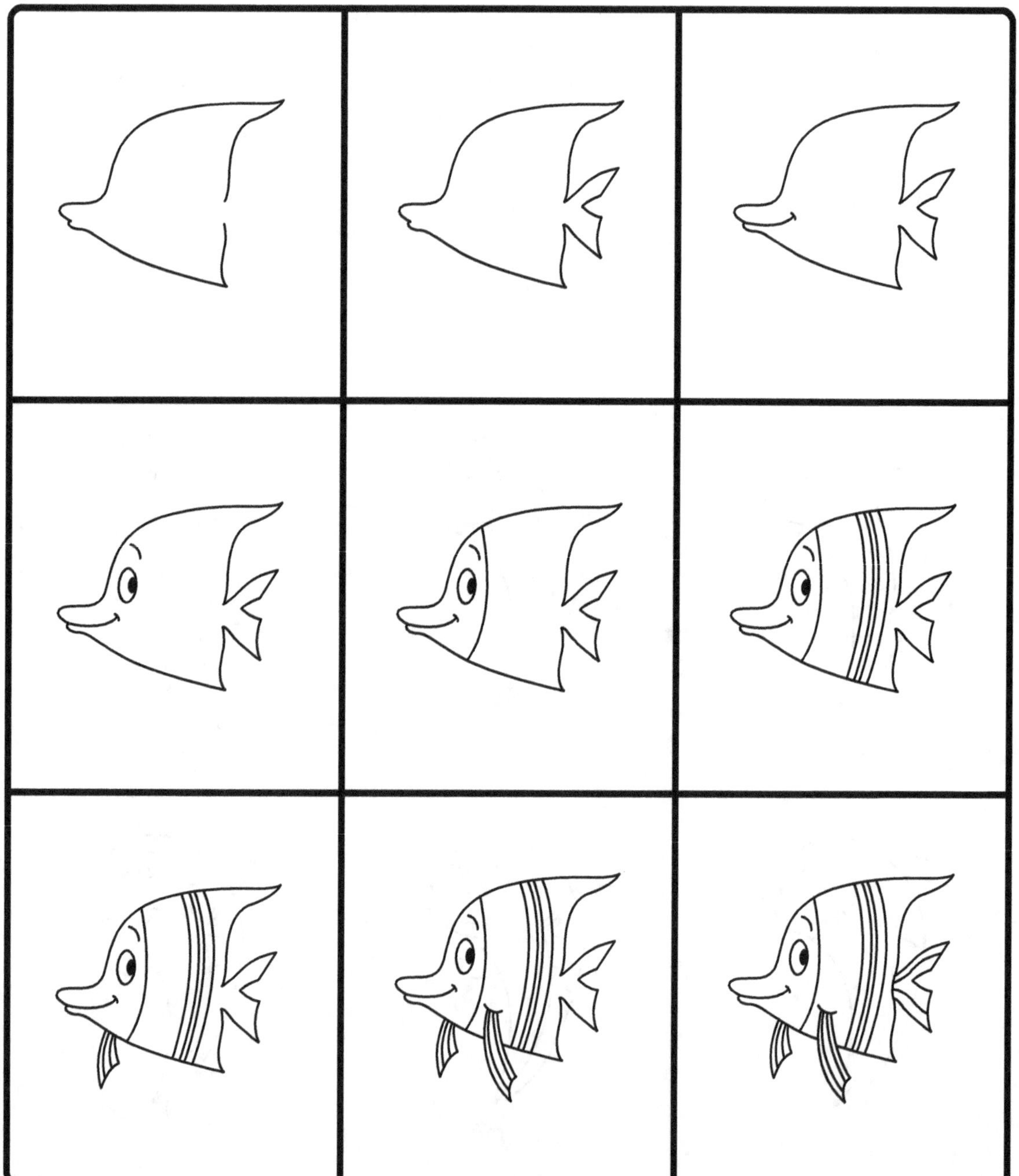

SEAHORSE

FUN FACT:
THE DAD'S HAVE THE BABIES!

SPECIES:
47

JOKE:
WHAT KIND OF HORSE CAN
NEVER DROWN?
A SEAHORSE.

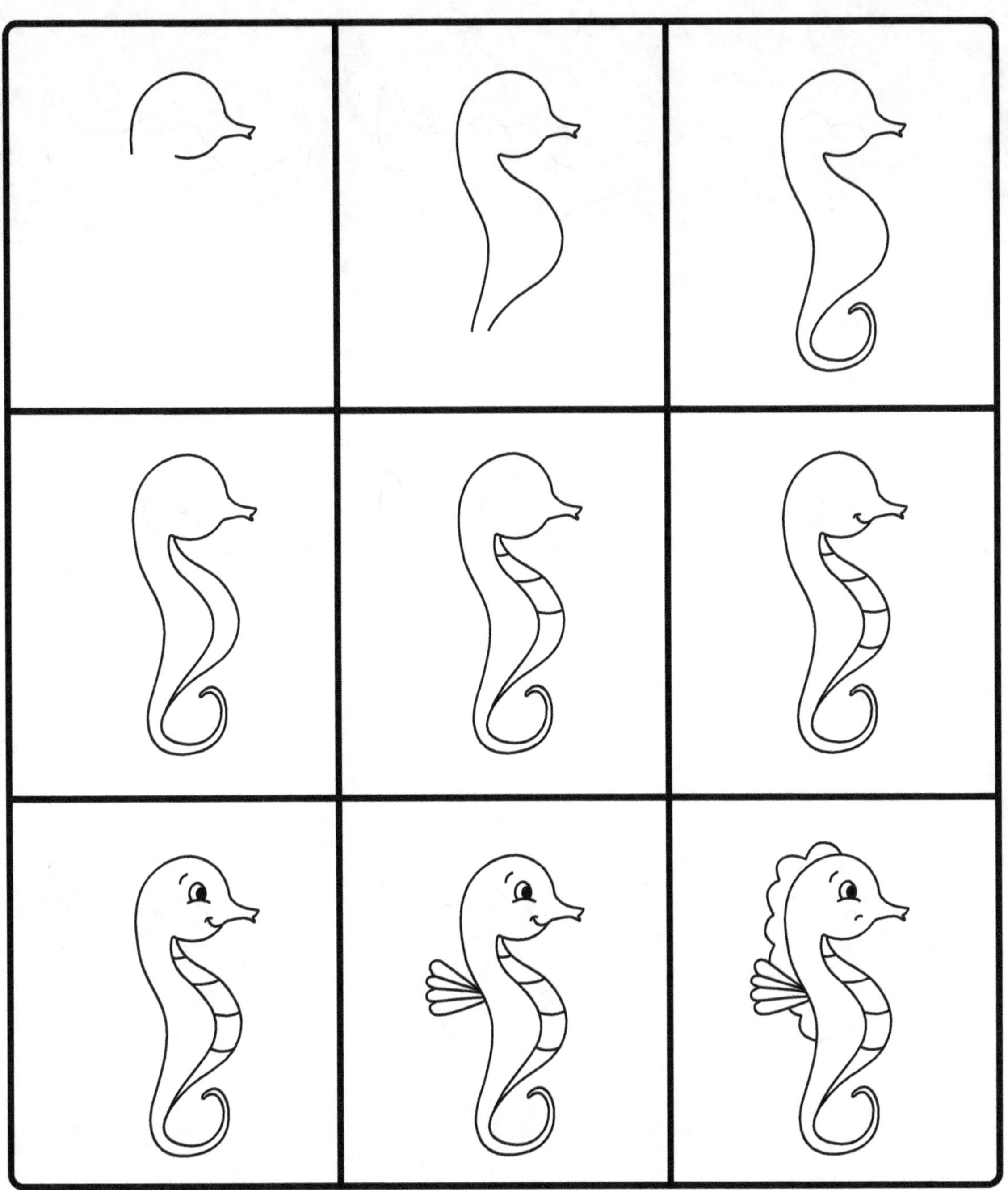

STINGRAY

FUN FACT:
JAPANESE USE THEIR SKINS
TO MAKE SWORDS.

SPECIES:
220

JOKE:
WHAT DO YOU GET WHEN YOU
CROSS A STINGRAY AND A
SKUNK?
A STINK-RAY.

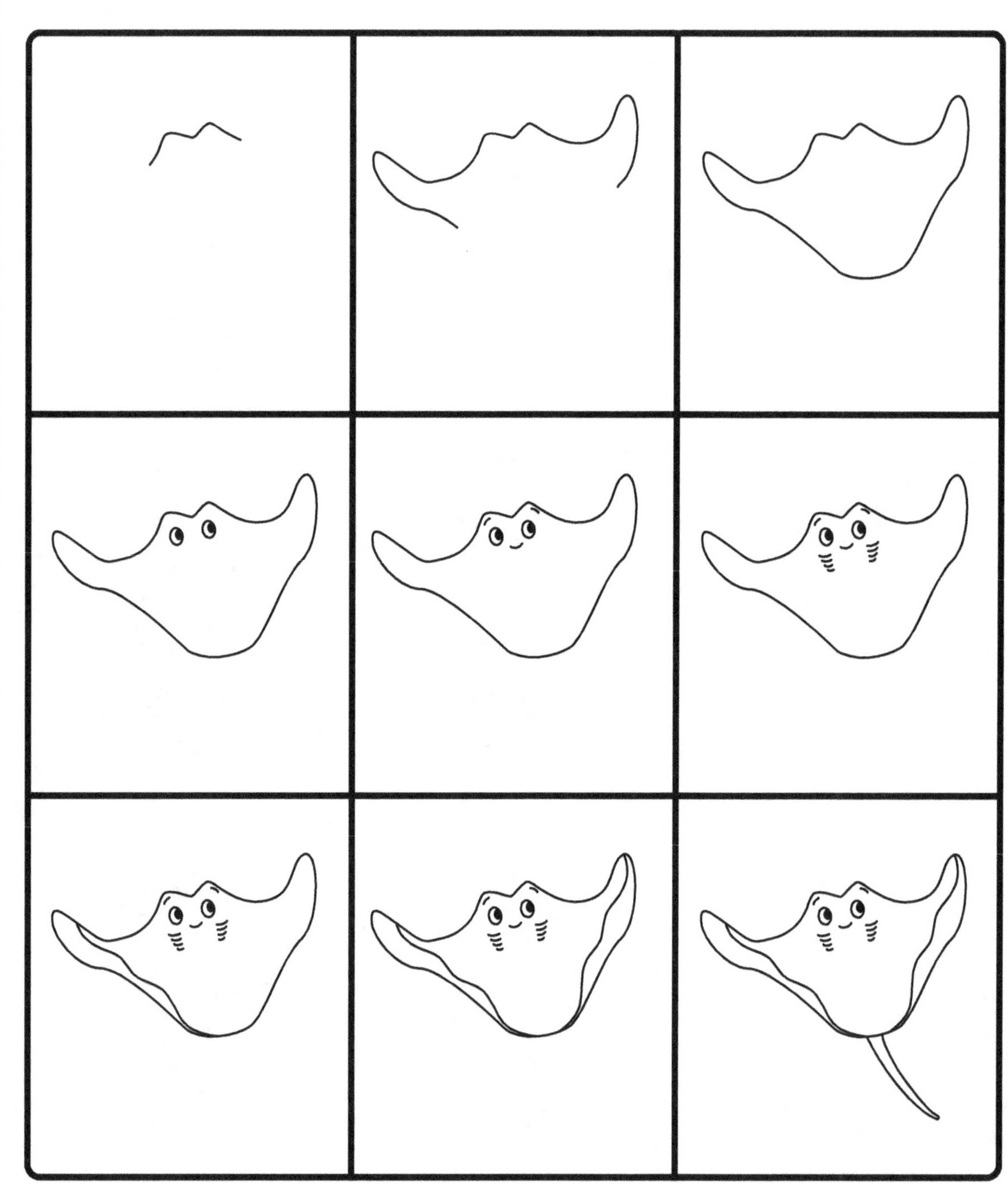

REPTILES

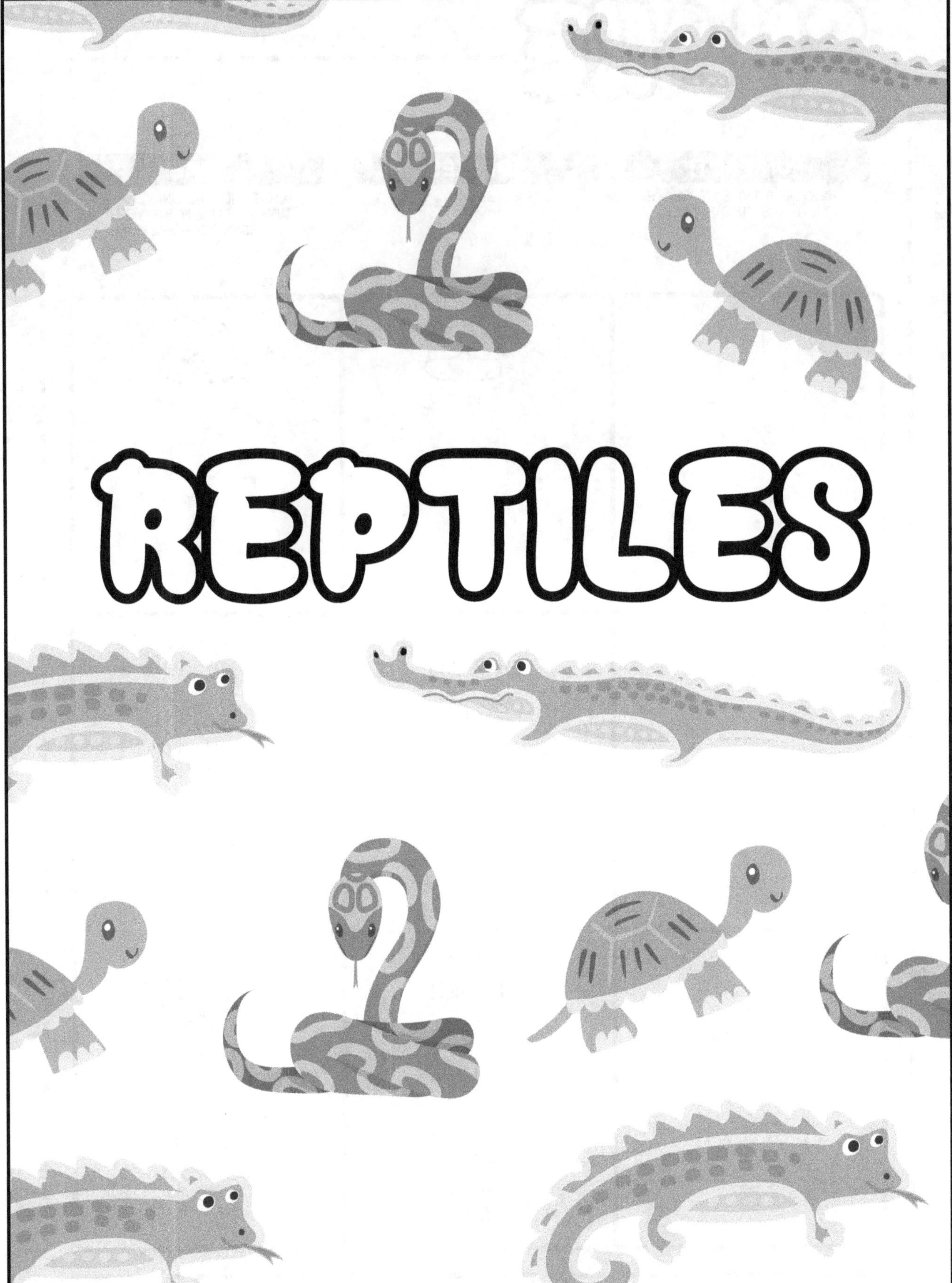

SNAKE

FUN FACT:
THERE IS A TYPE OF SNAKE
THAT HAS TWO HEADS!

SPECIES:
3600

JOKE:
WHAT DID THE SNAKE SAY
WHEN AFTER IT BIT YOU?
SSSSSSSSSORRY!

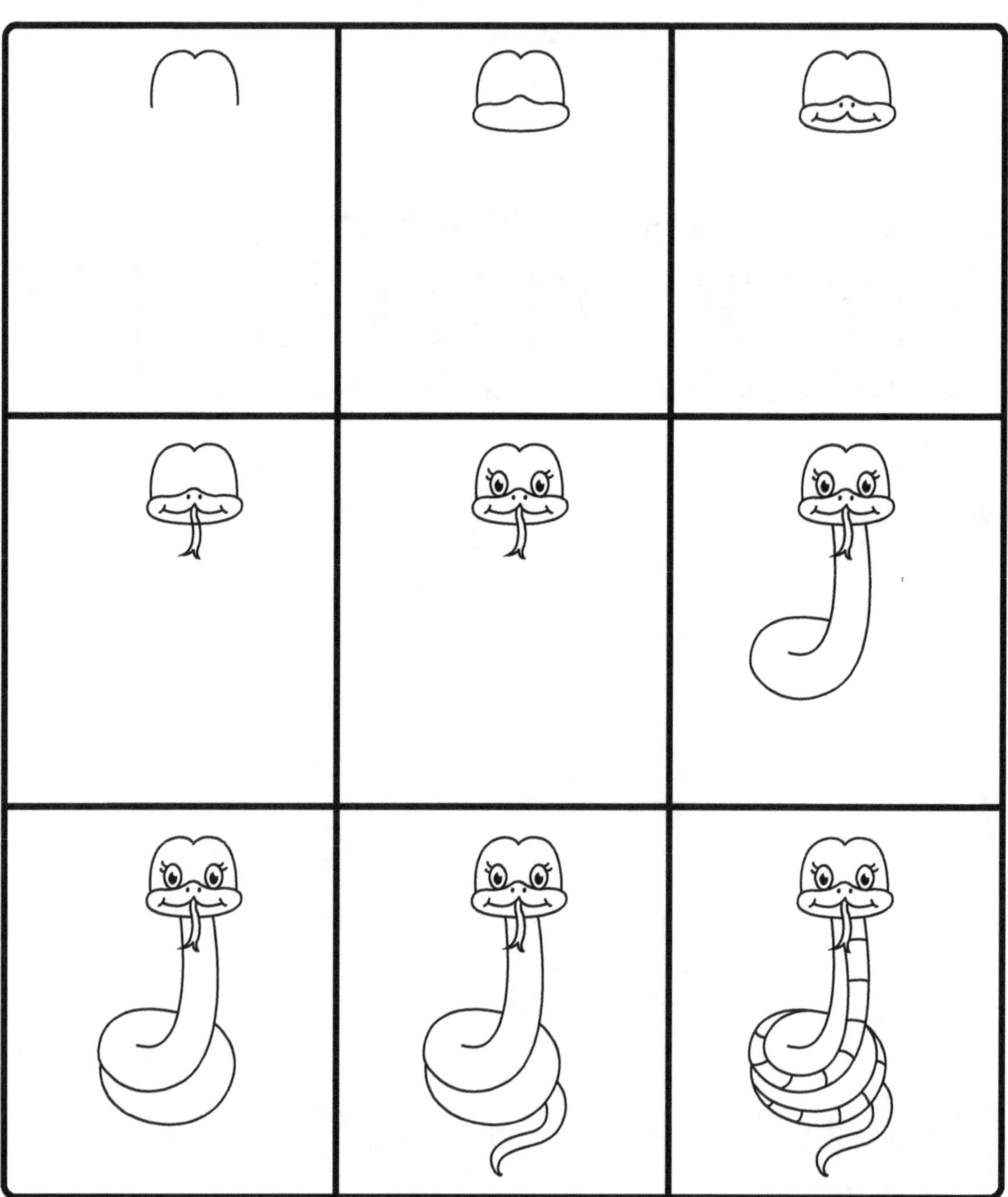

CROCODILE

FUN FACT:
CROCODILES REALLY DO CRY TEARS! IT HAPPENS WHEN THEY EAT AND SWALLOW TOO MUCH AIR, MAKING THEIR EYES WATER.

SPECIES:
24

JOKE:
HOW DOES A CROCODILE WAKE UP HIS FRIENDS? CROC-O-DOODLE-DOO!

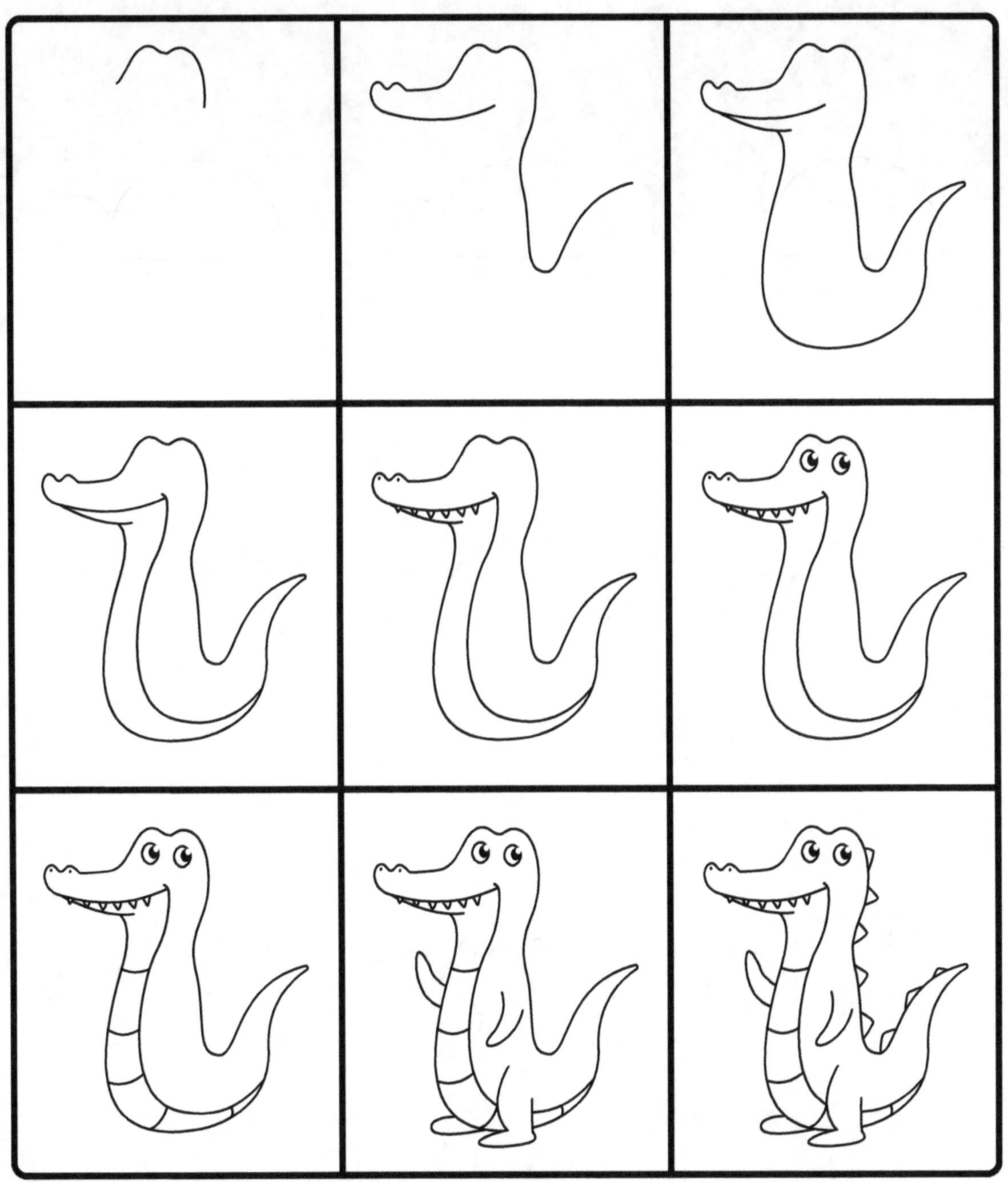

TURTLE

FUN FACT:
TURTLES HAVE THREE EARS!

SPECIES:
356

JOKE:
WHY DO TURTLES LOVE
PHONES?
TO TAKE SHELLFIES!

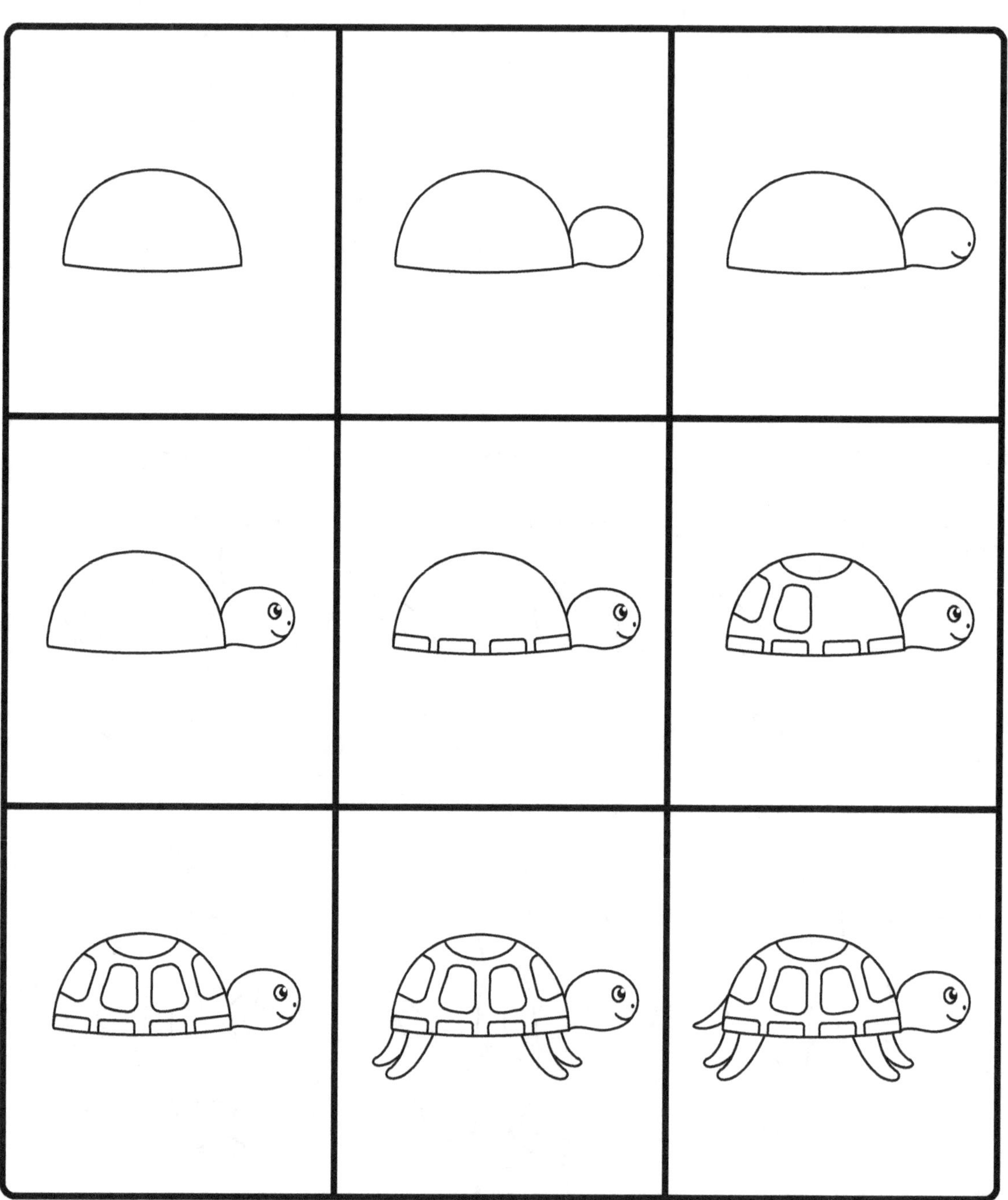

LIZARD

FUN FACT:

LIZARDS LOSE THEIR TAILS
WHEN THEY FEEL THREAT-
ENED. THEY DO GROW THEM
BACK THOUGH!

SPECIES:

6000+

JOKE:

WHAT DO LIZARDS LOVE TO
DO IN THEIR SPARE TIME?
RETAIL SHOPPING.

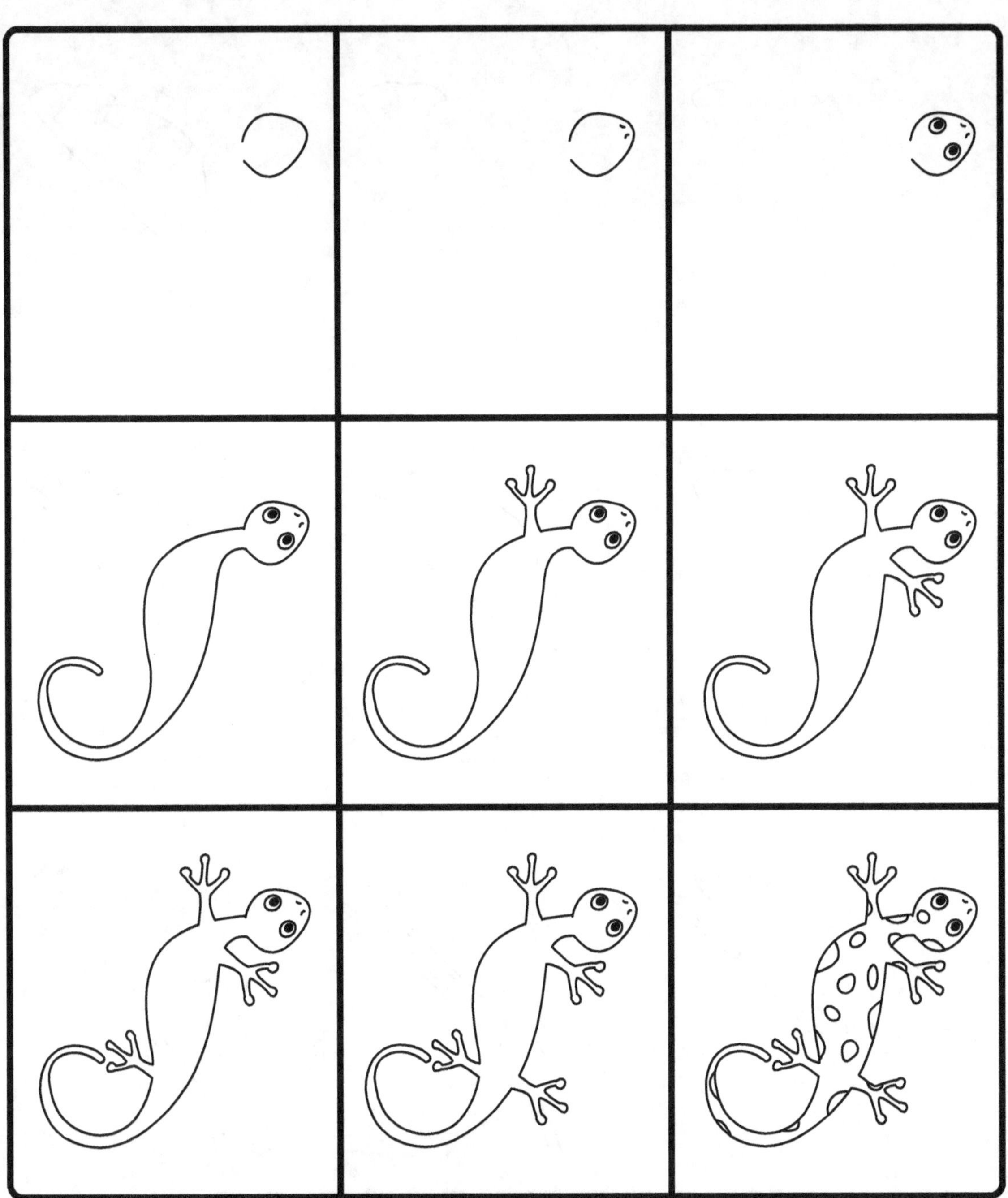

CHAMELEON

FUN FACT:
CHAMELEONS CAN FLICK OUT
THEIR TONGUE TWICE THE
LENGTH OF THEIR BODIES.

SPECIES:
150+

JOKE:
WHERE DO LIZARDS GO FOR
ENTERTAINMENT?
TO SEE A STAND-UP
CHAMELEON.

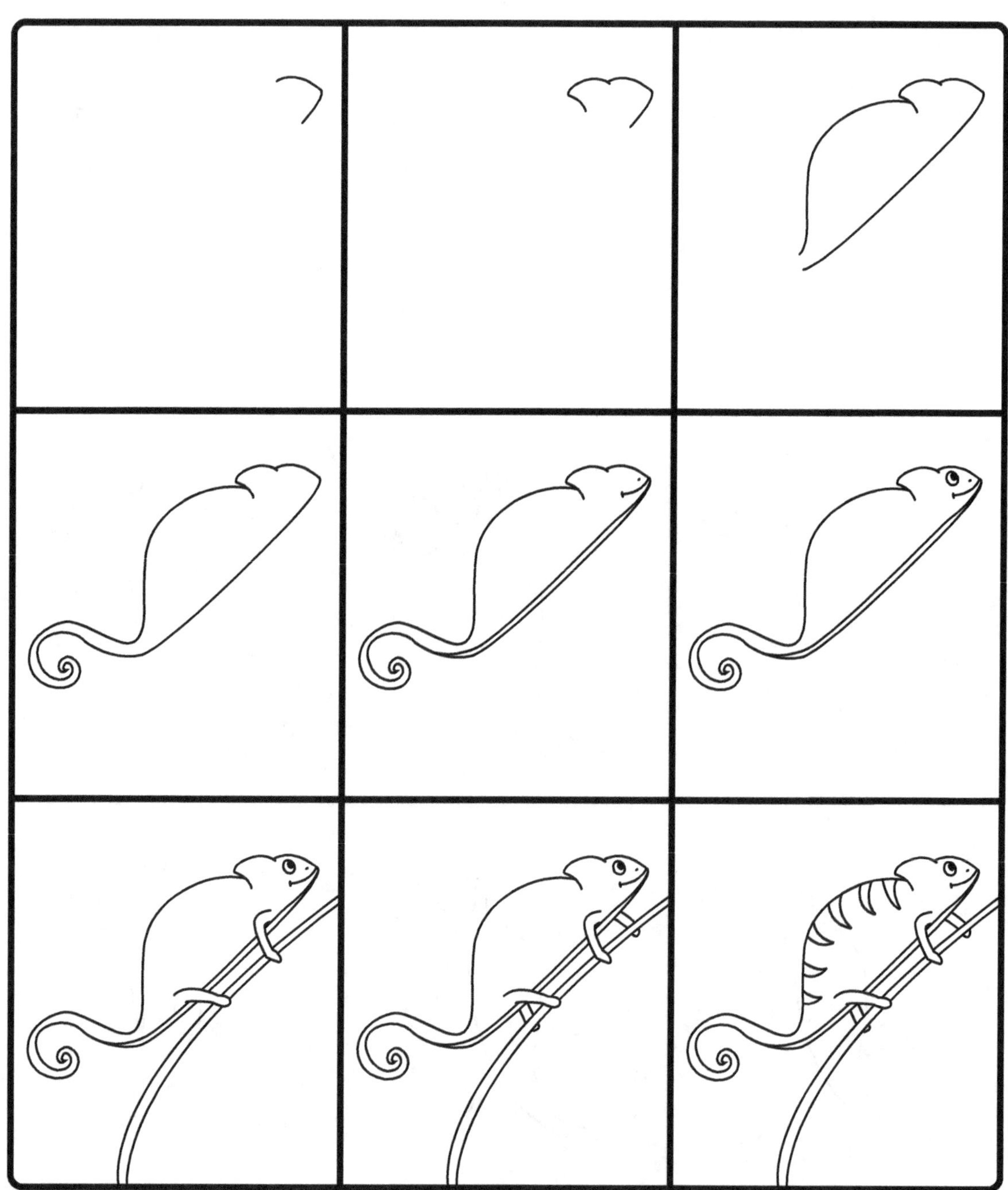

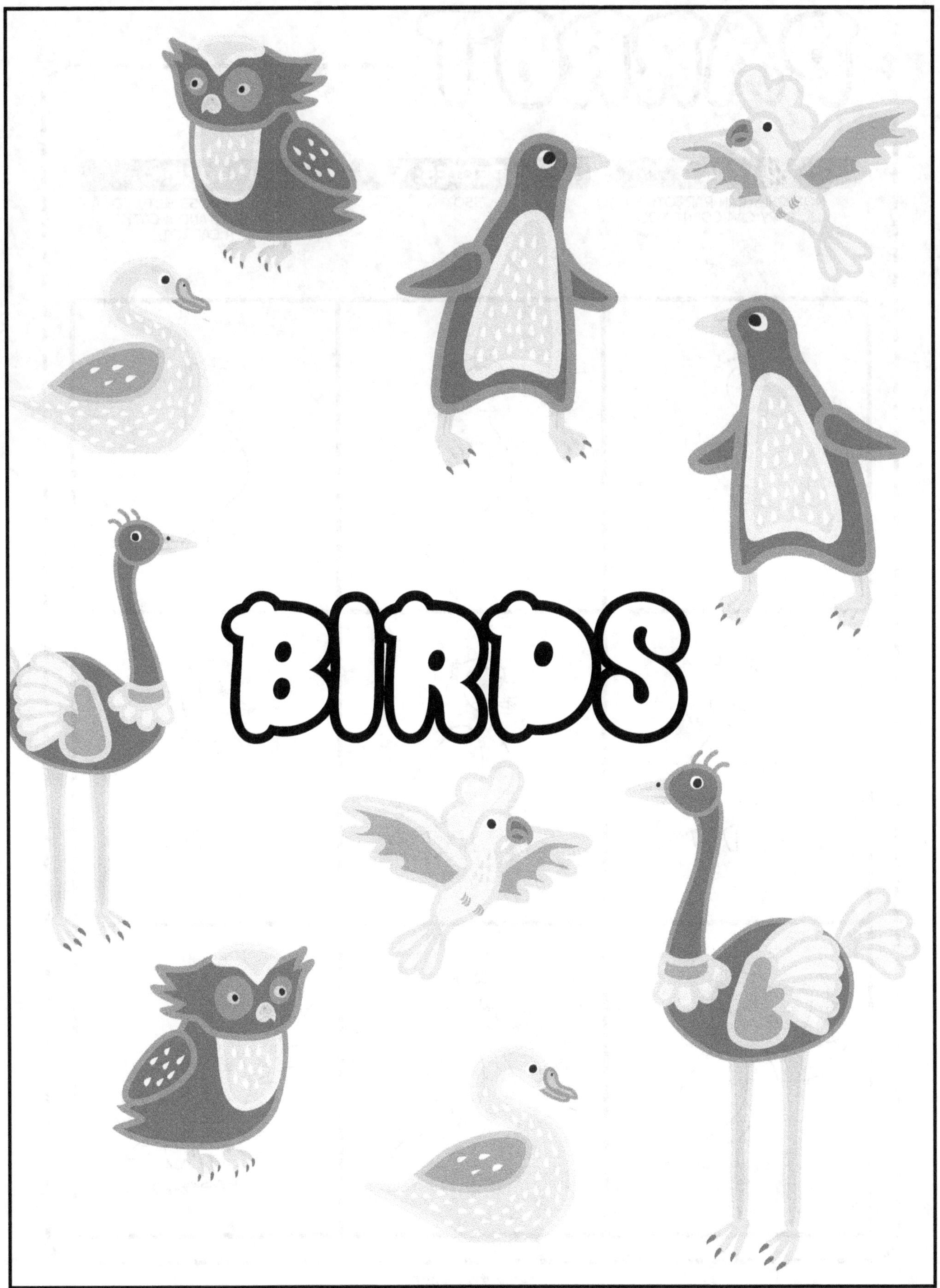
BIRDS

PARROT

FUN FACT:
NOT ONLY CAN PARROTS
TALK, THEY CAN COUNT TOO!

SPECIES:
350

JOKE:
WHAT'S A CROSS BETWEEN A
PARROT AND A CAT?
A CARROT.

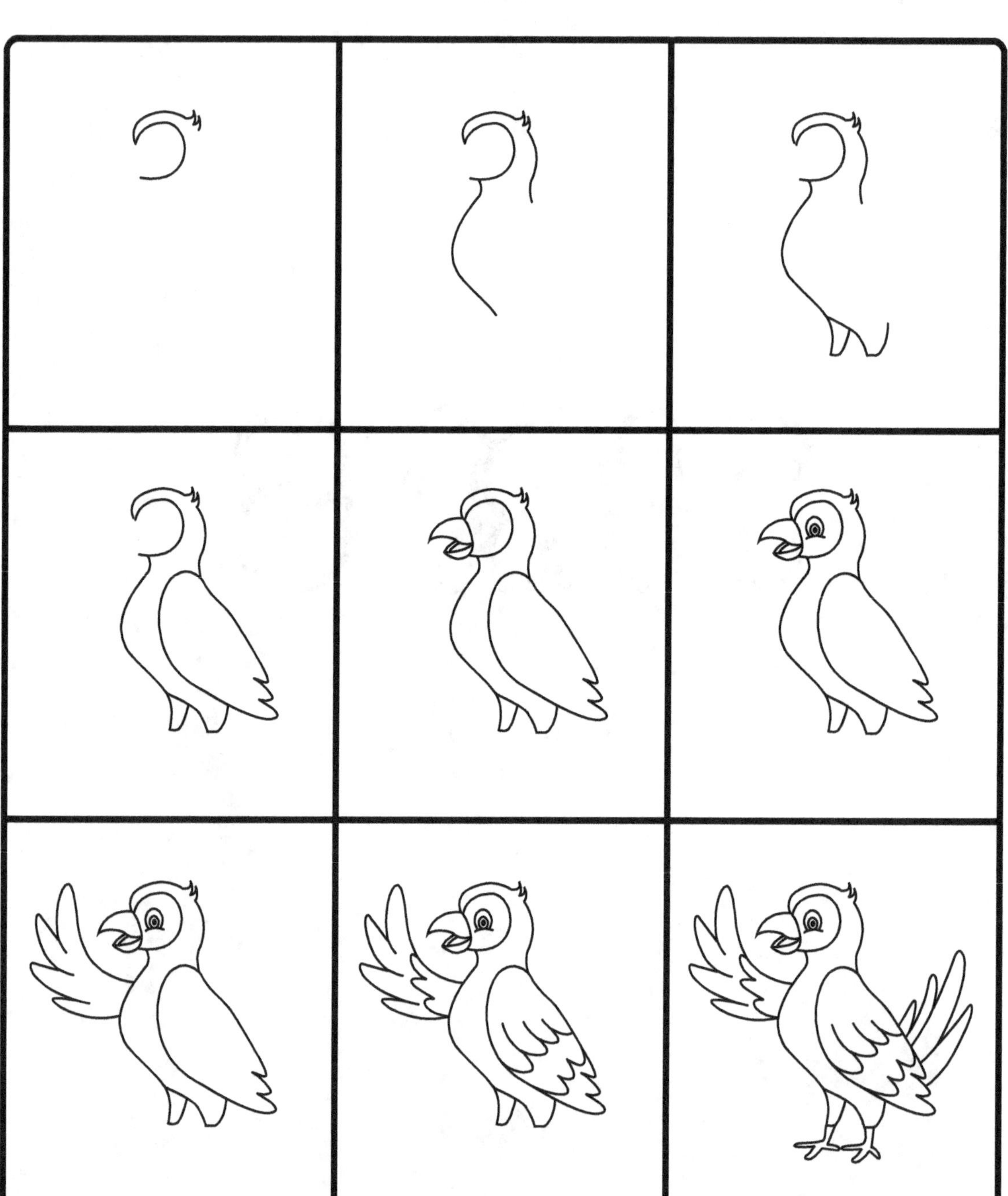

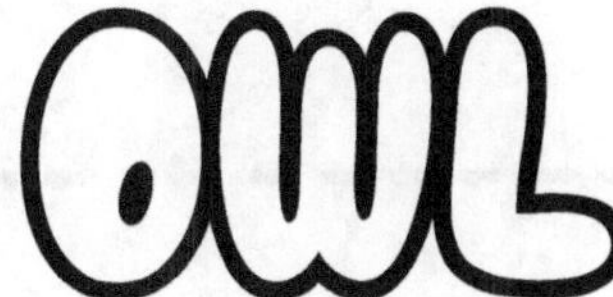

OWL

FUN FACT:
WHEN OWLETS ARE BORN
THEY HAVE A SPECIAL 'EGG
TOOTH' TOOL THAT ENABLES
THEM TO GET OUT OF THEIR
SHELL.

SPECIES:
250

JOKE:
WHAT DO YOU CALL AN OWL
WHO KEEPS ESCAPING?
HOODINI.

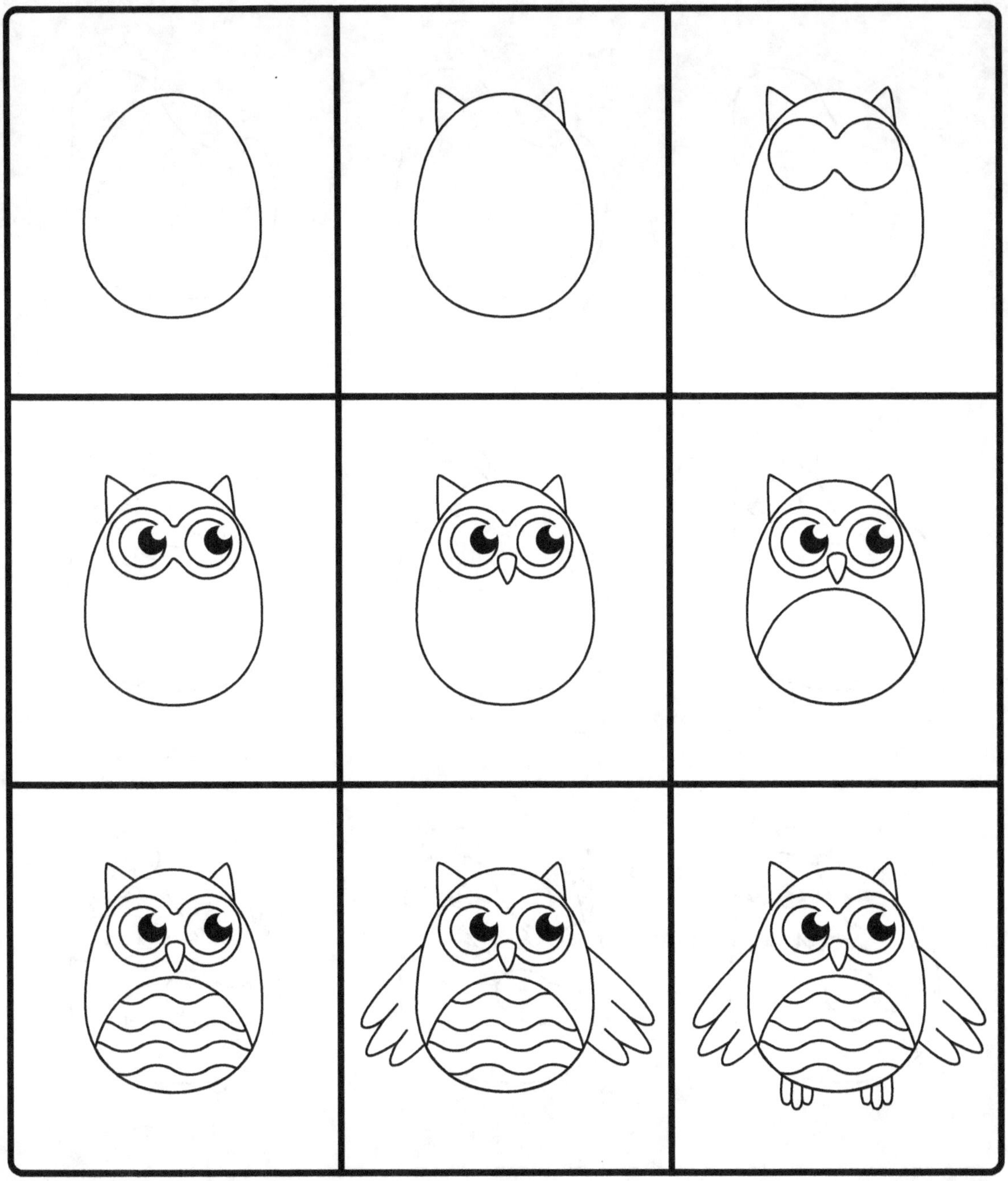

CHICKEN

FUN FACT:
UNLIKE MANY ANIMALS,
CHICKENS CAN SEE ALL THE
COLORS IN THE WORLD.

SPECIES:
500+

JOKE:
WHAT DO YOU CALL A
BIRD THAT'S SCARED OF
EVERYTHING?
A CHICKEN.

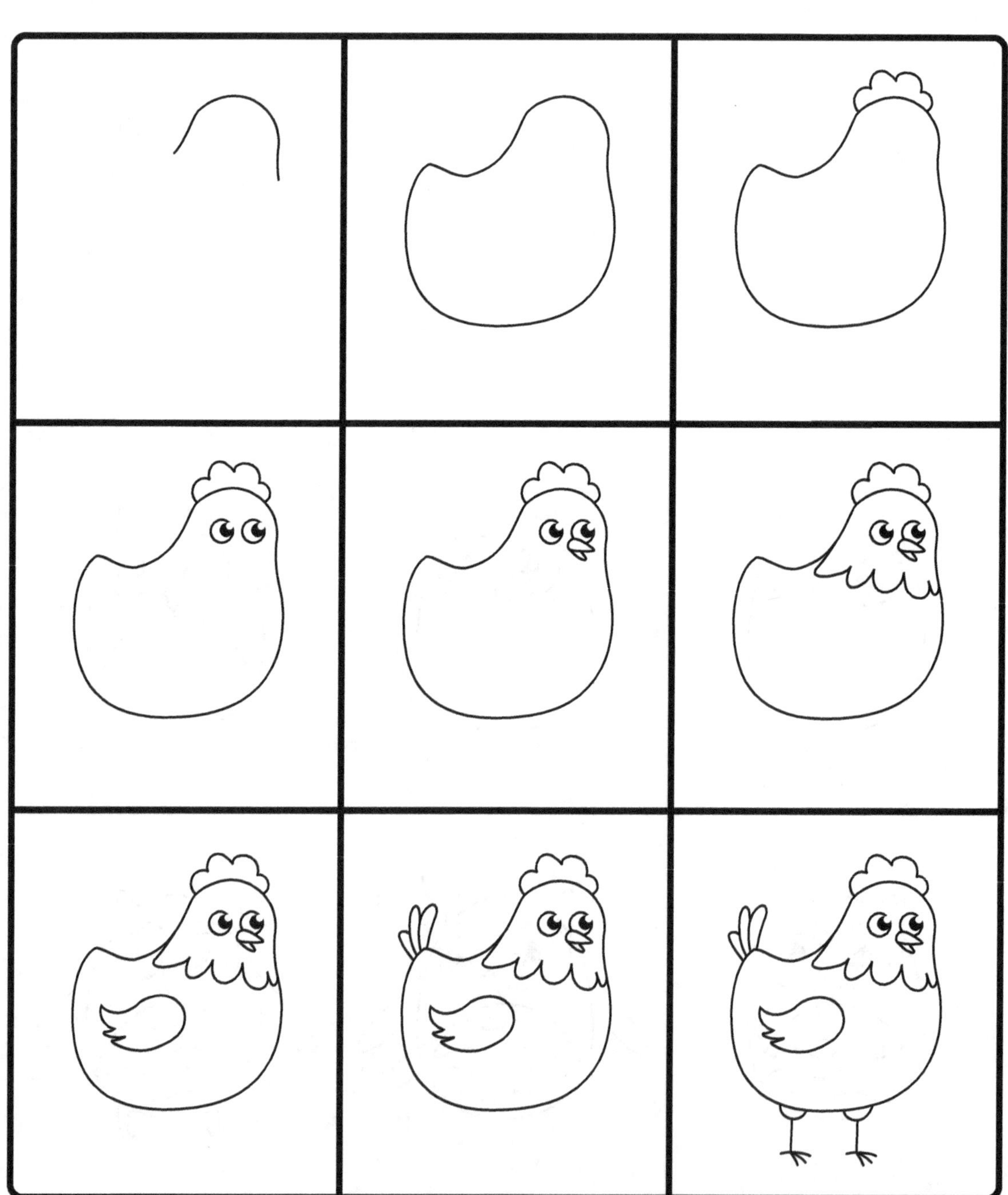

TOUCAN

FUN FACT:
TOUCANS NOT ONLY EAT
FRUIT, BUT MEAT TOO.

SPECIES:
42

JOKE:
HOW MANY TROPICAL BIRDS
DOES IT TAKE TO CHANGE A
LIGHTBULB?
TOUCAN!

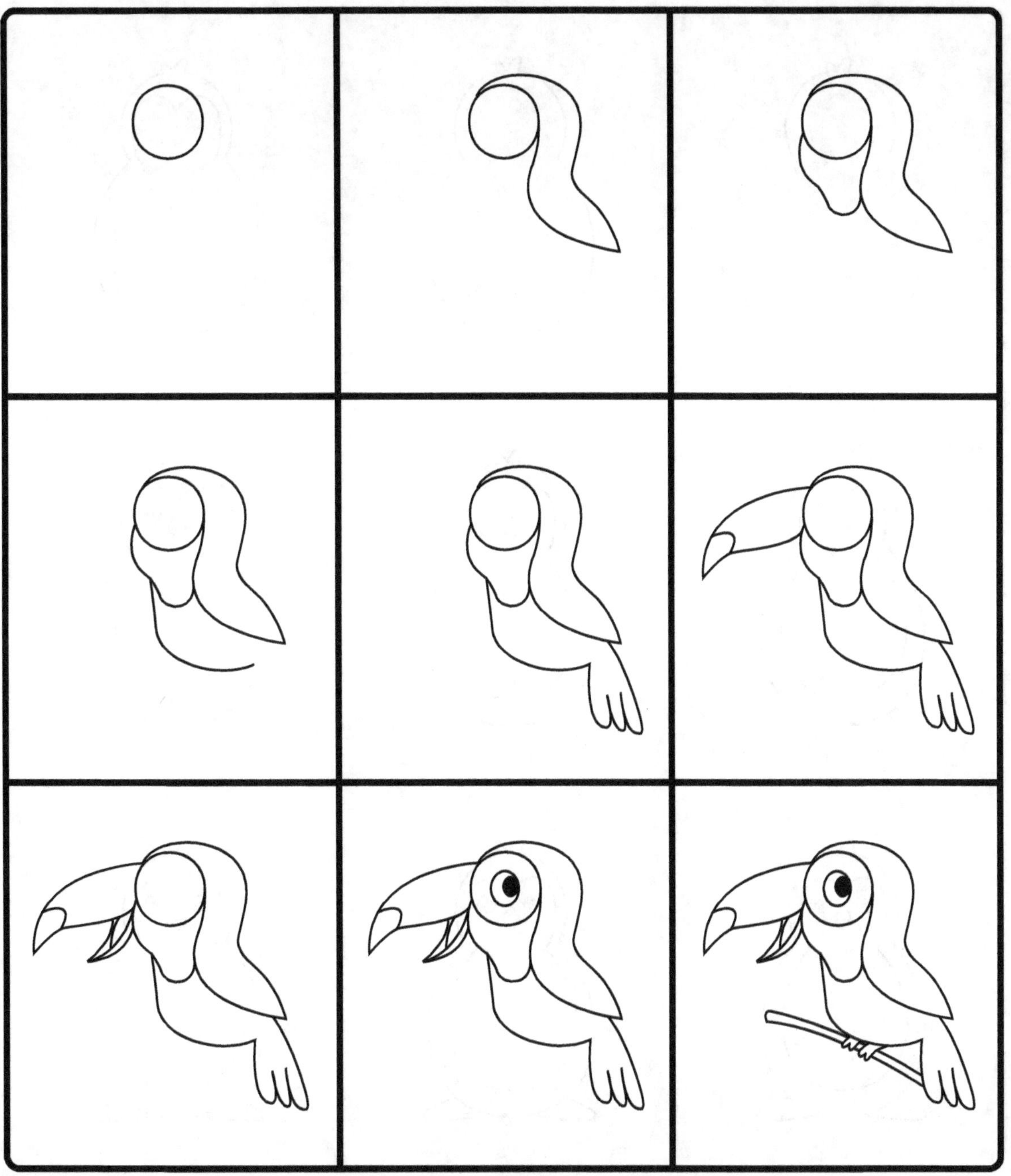

PENGUIN

THEIR FASTEST WAY OF GETTING AROUND IS BY SLIDING ON THE SNOW, LIKE TOBOGGANING.

18

WHAT'S BLACK WHITE AND RED ALL OVER? A PENGUIN TRYING TO GET A SUNTAN.

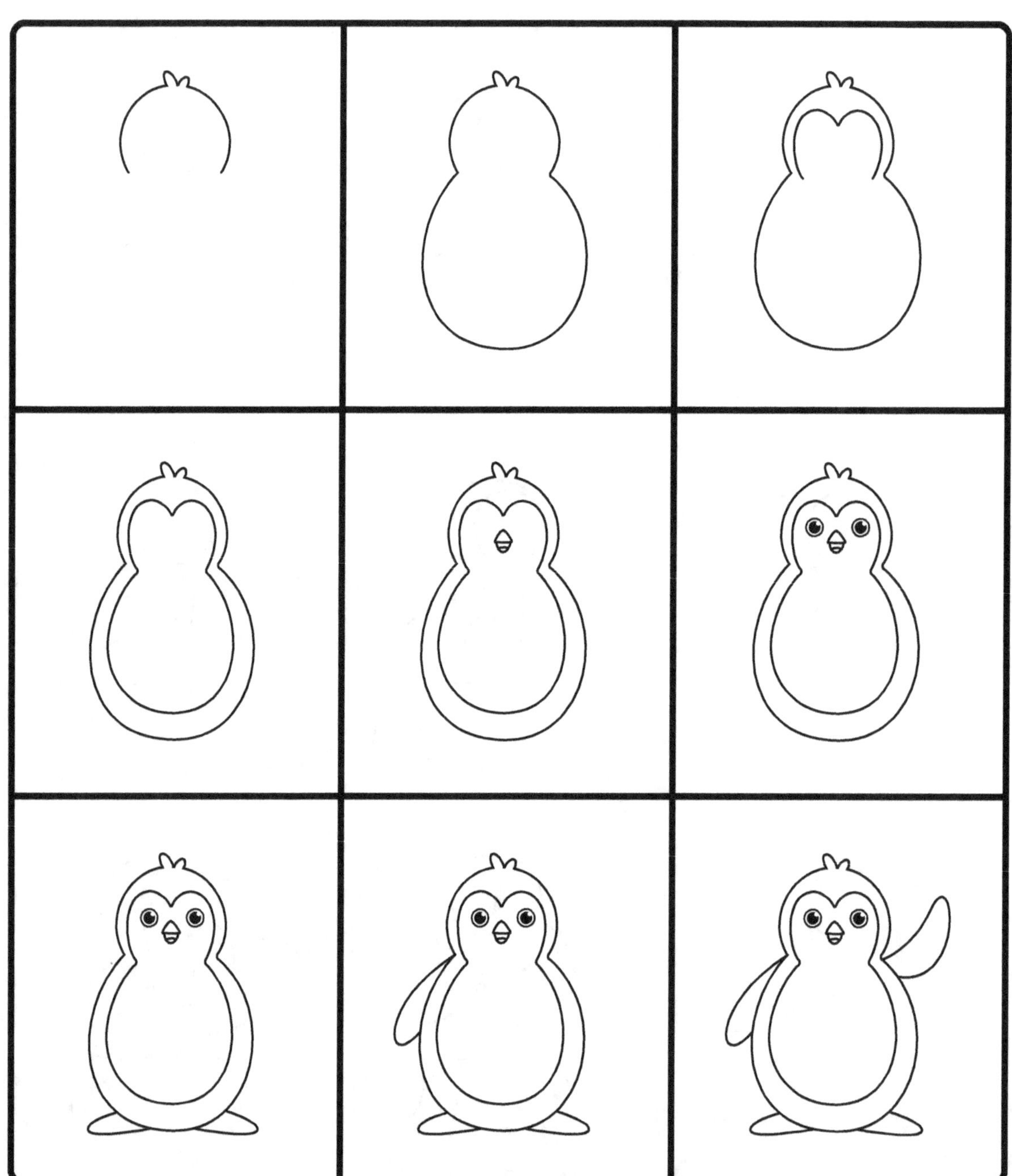

OSTRICH

FUN FACT:

OSTRICHES HAVE THE LARG-
EST EYES OF ALL LAND
ANIMALS.

SPECIES:

2

JOKE:

WHY DO OSTRICHES LOVE THE
BEACH?
SO THEY CAN STICK THEIR
HEAD IN THE SAND.

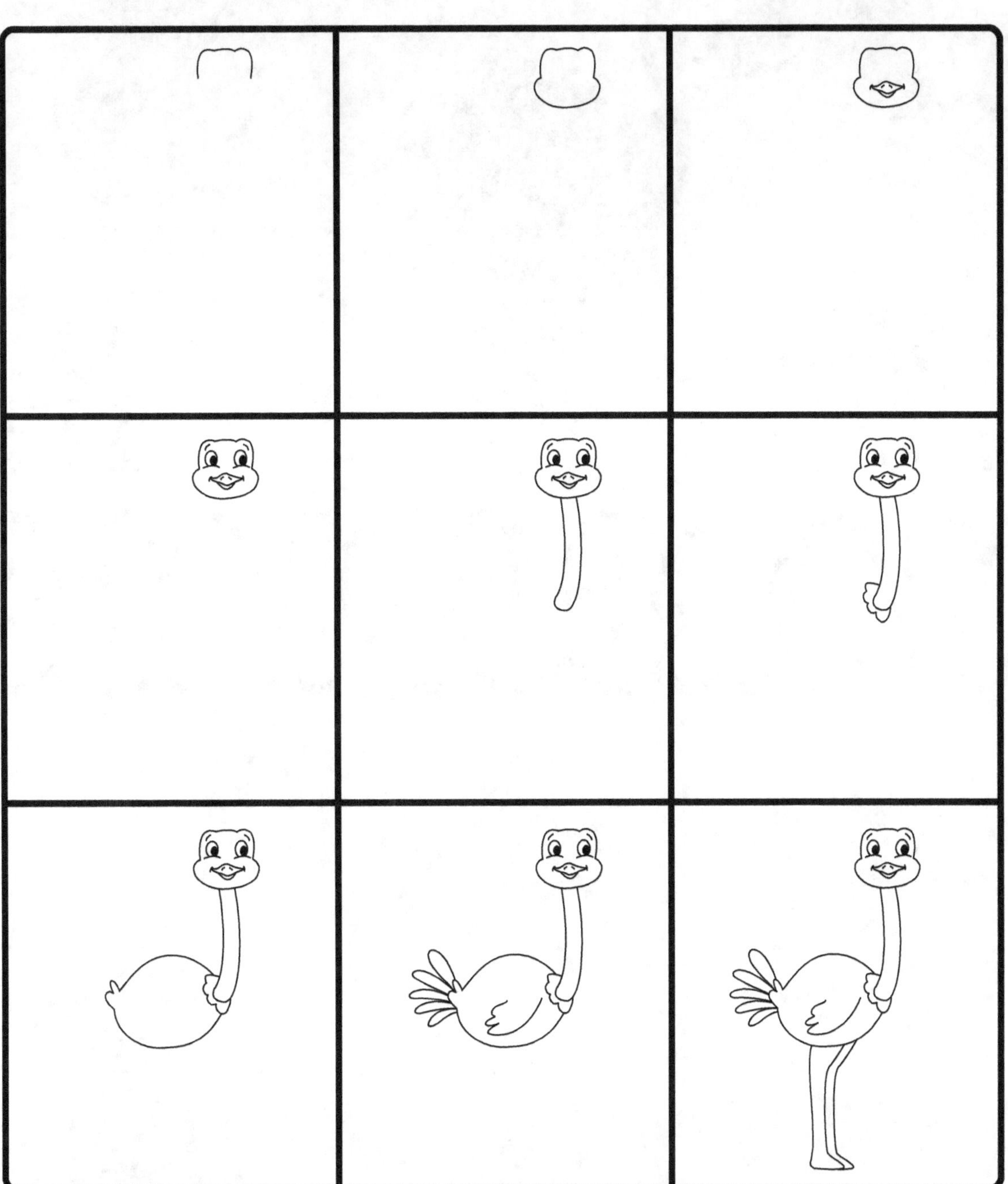

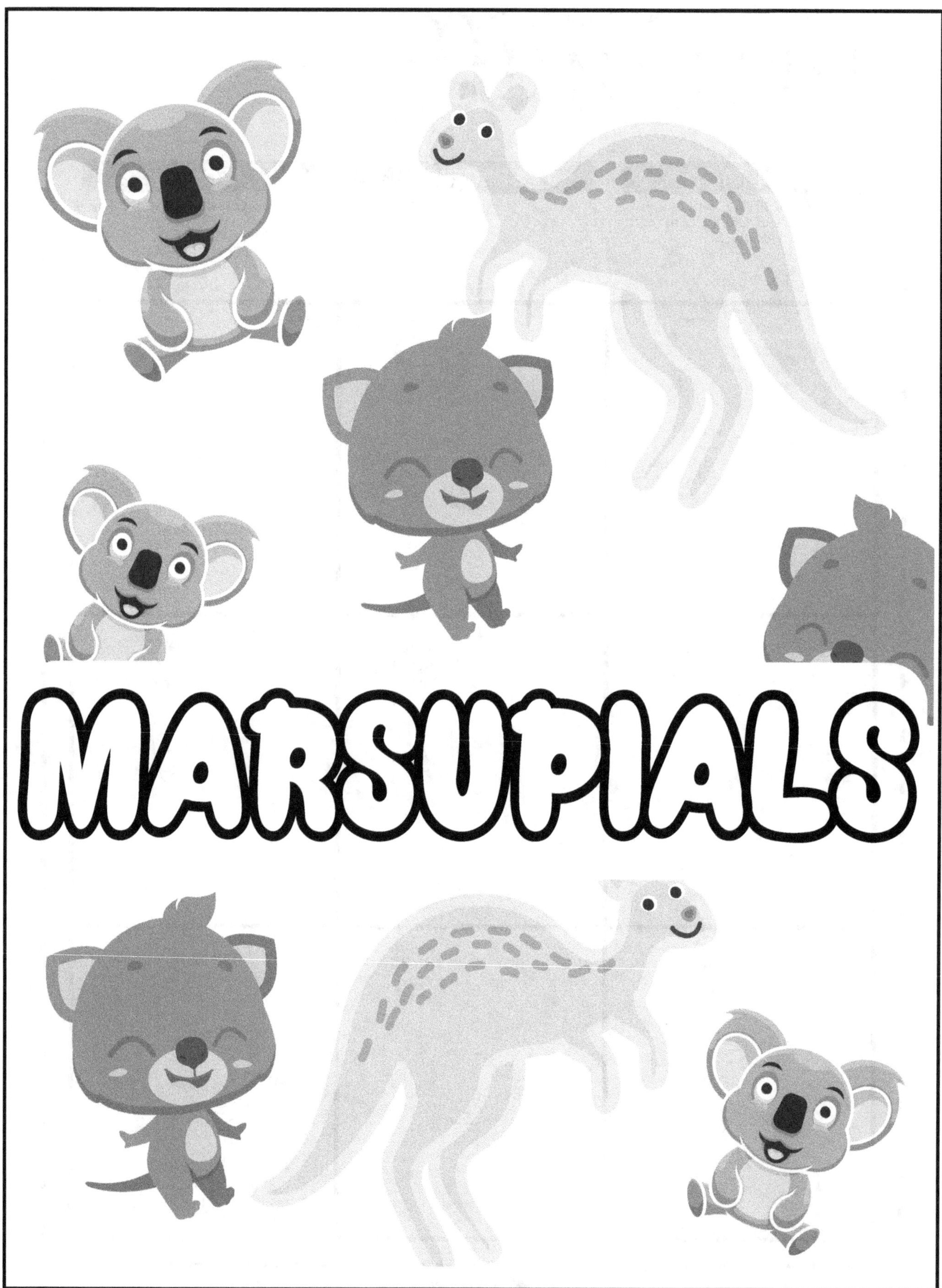

MARSUPIALS

KANGAROO

FUN FACT:
THEY USE THEIR TAIL AS A FIFTH LEG.

SPECIES:
4

JOKE:
WHAT HAPPENED WHEN THE KANGAROO BROKE HIS LEG? HE WENT TO HOPSITAL.

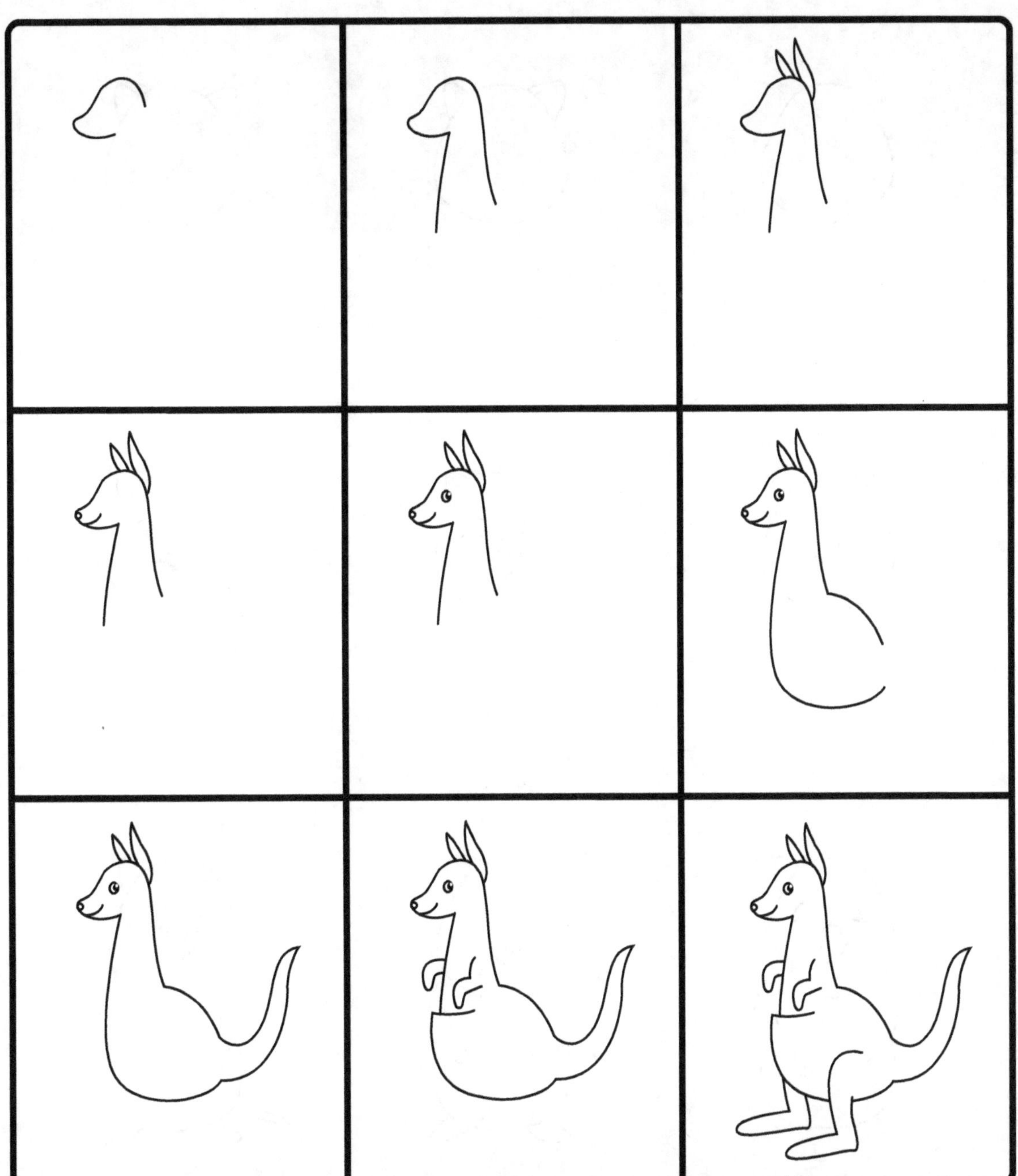

QUOKKA

FUN FACT:
THEY ARE OFTEN SMILING,
WHICH MEANS THEY ARE HOT!

SPECIES:
1

JOKE:
WHAT DOES A QUOKKA
SAY FIRST THING IN THE
MORNING?
QUOKKA-DOODLE-DOO!

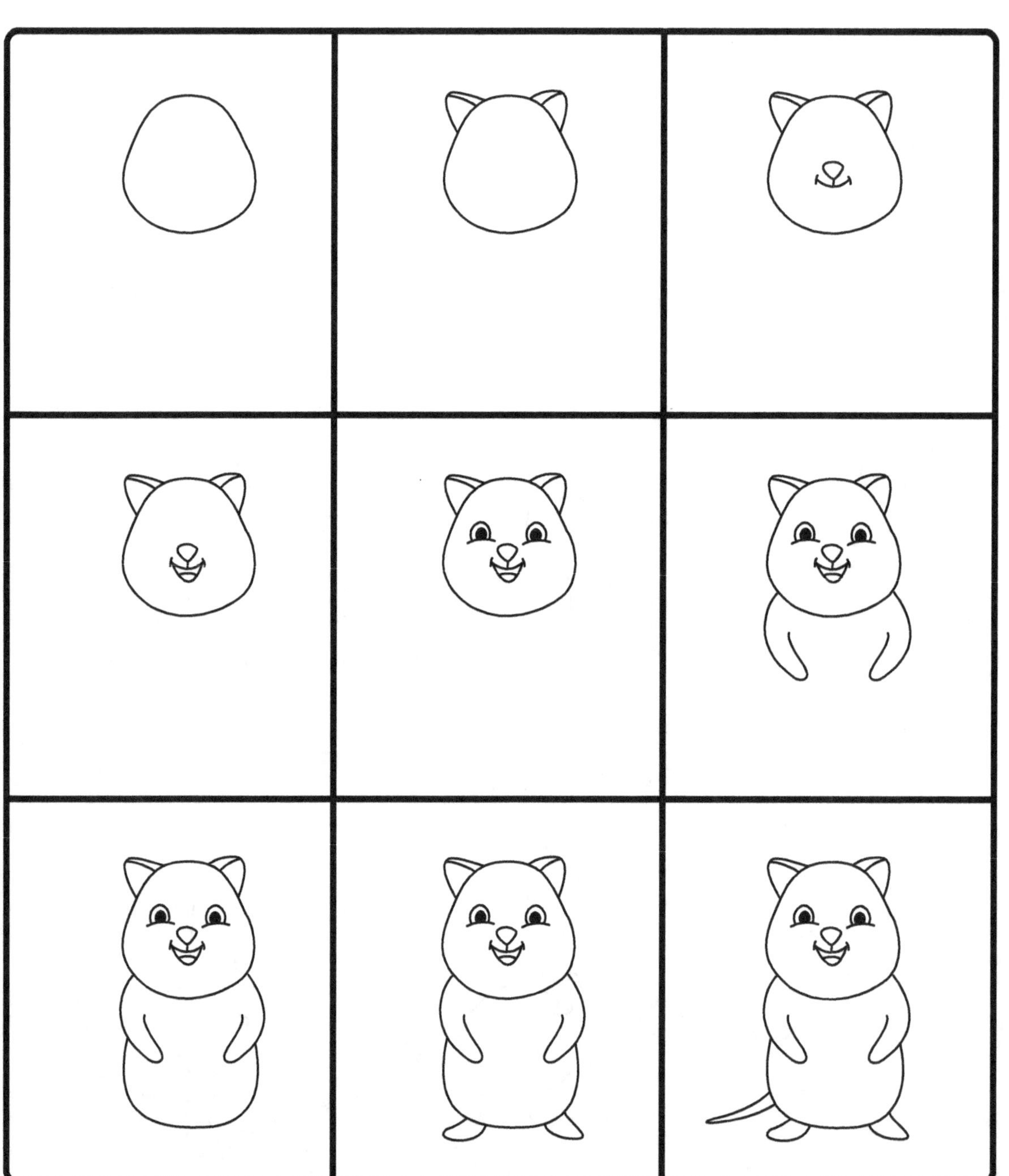

KOALA

FUN FACT:
THEY LOVE TO SLEEP - AND CAN SLEEP UP TO 20 HOURS A DAY!

SPECIES:
1

JOKE:
WHY DO KOALAS SLEEP ALL THE TIME?
IT'S TIRING BEING SO ADORABLE!

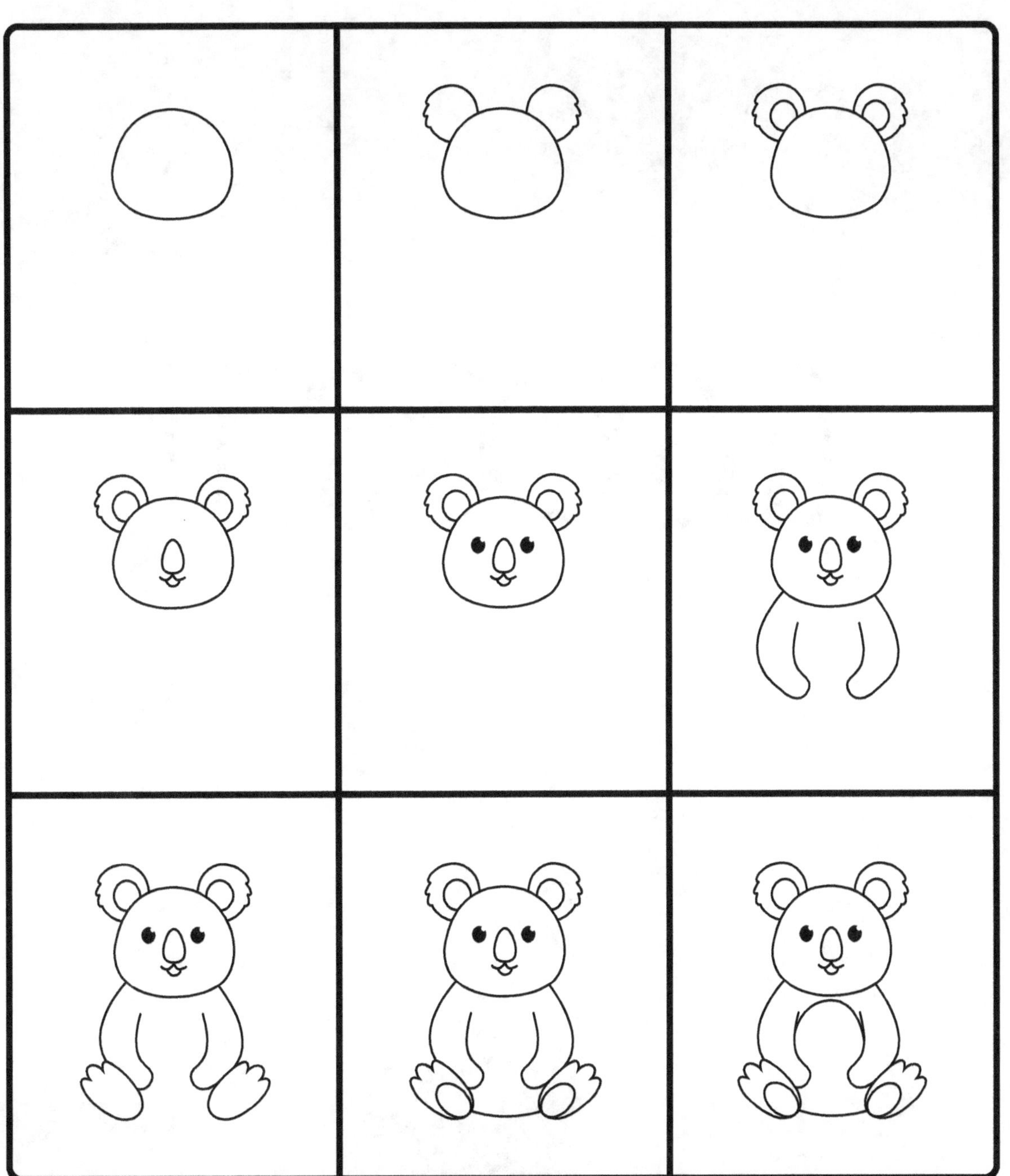

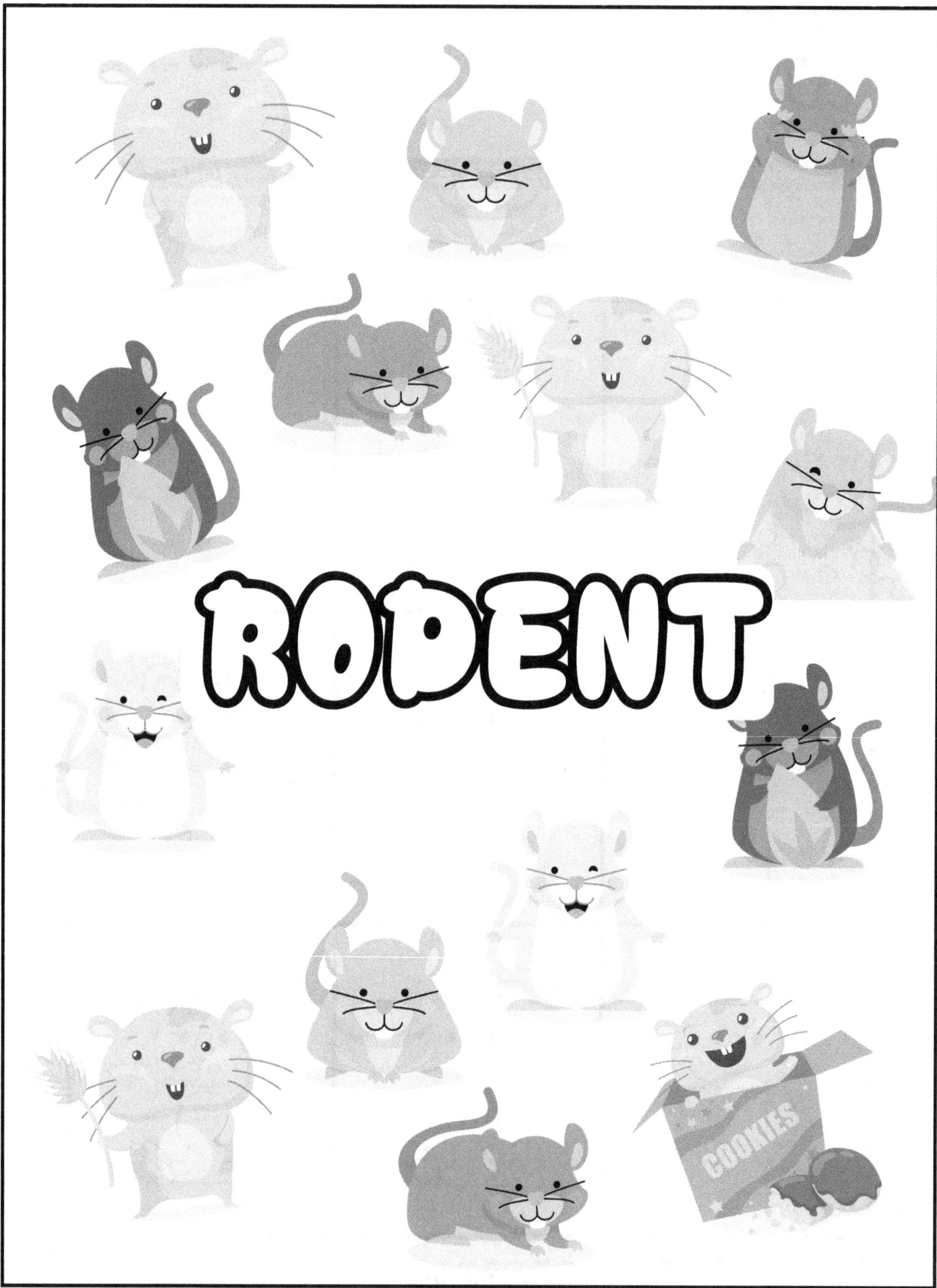
RODENT
COOKIES

MOUSE

FUN FACT:
MICE LAUGH WHEN THEY ARE TICKLED.

SPECIES:
1100

JOKE:
WHY DO YOU NEED TO OIL A MOUSE? BECAUSE THEY ARE SO SQUEAKY.

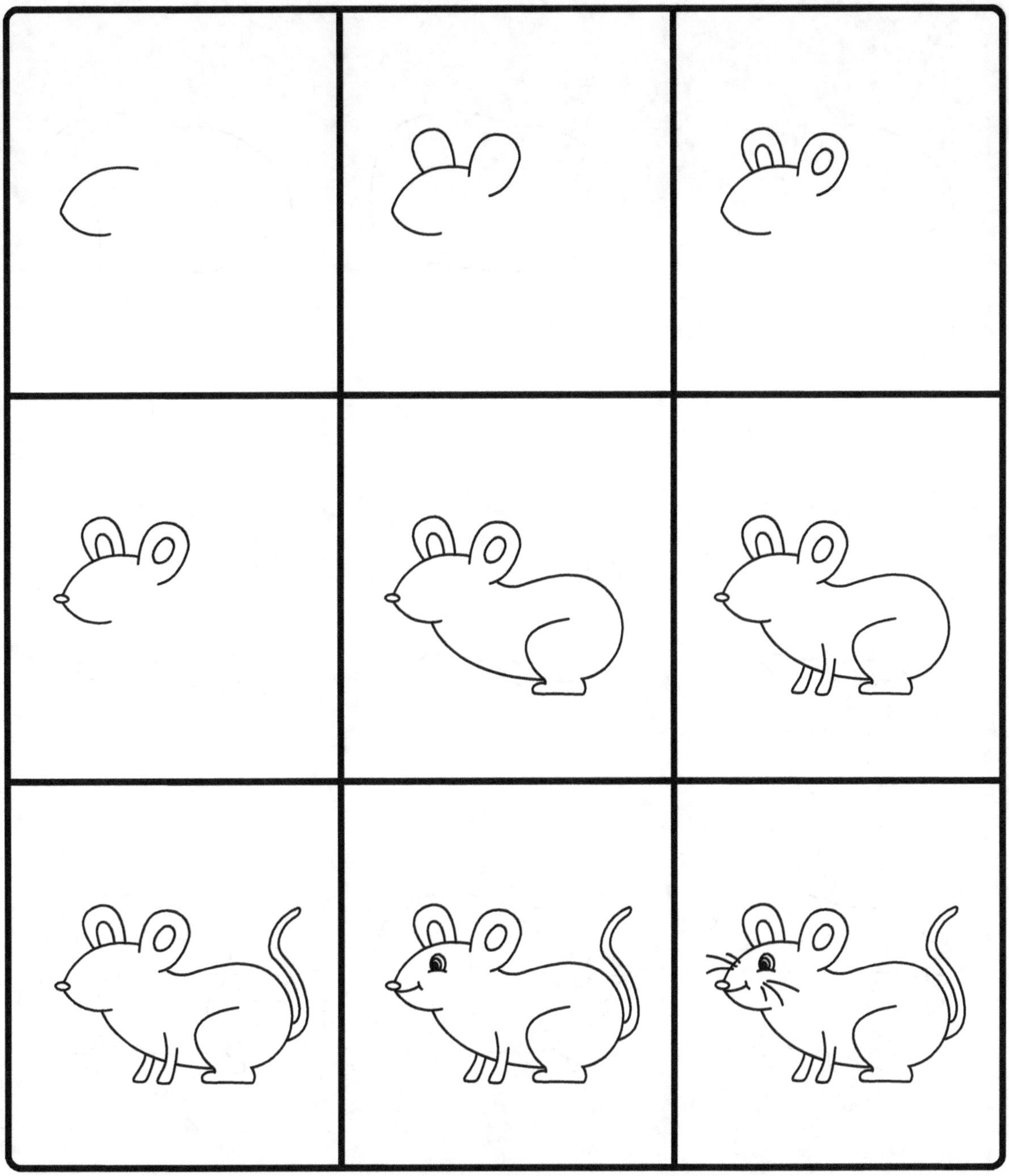

GUINEA PIG

FUN FACT:
GUINEA PIGS JUMP IN THE AIR
WHEN THEY ARE EXCITED. IT'S
CALLED 'POPCORNING!'

SPECIES:
13

JOKE:
WHY DID THE GUINEA PIG QUIT
HIS JOB?
THE SALARY WAS NOT
ENOUGH.

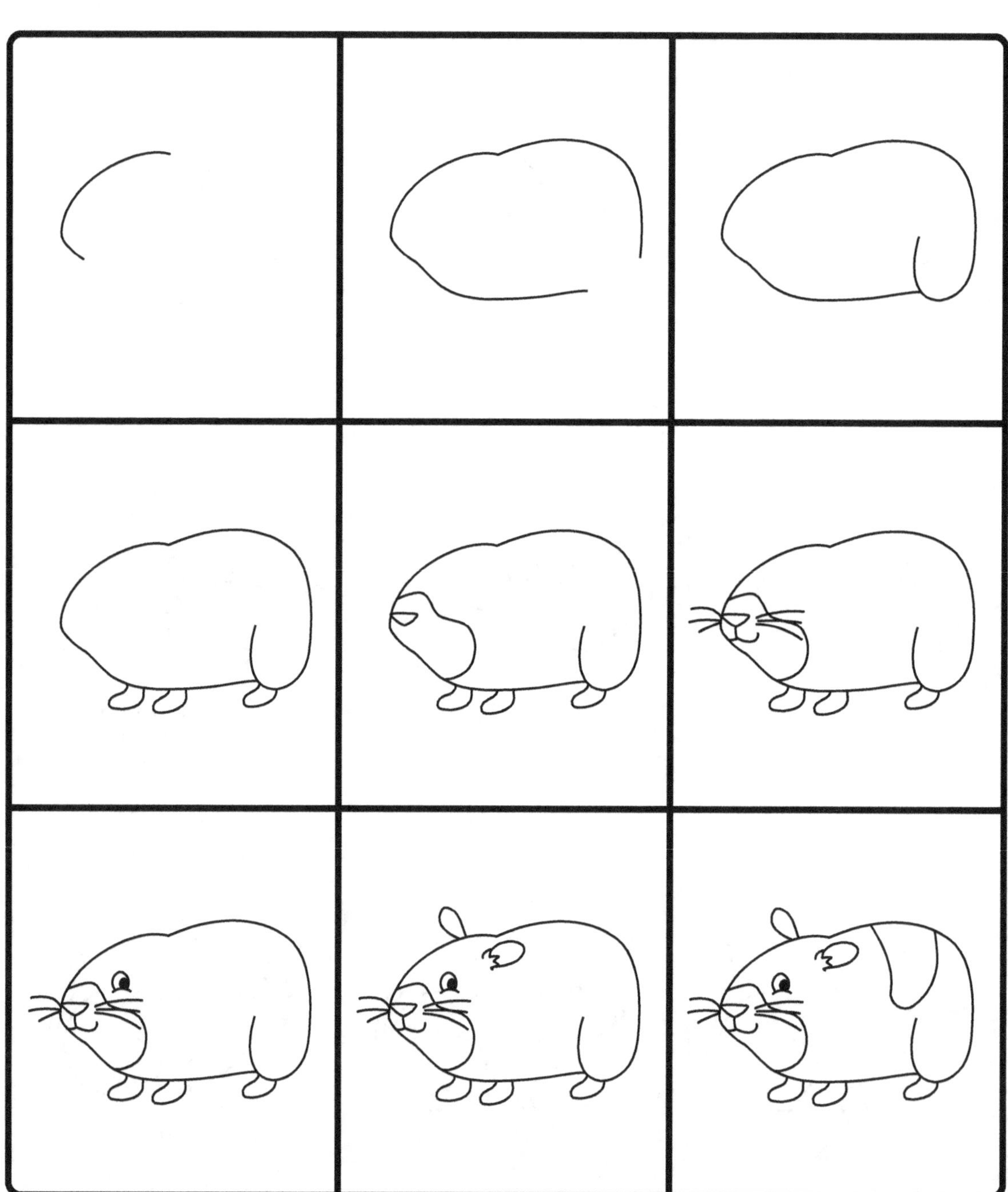

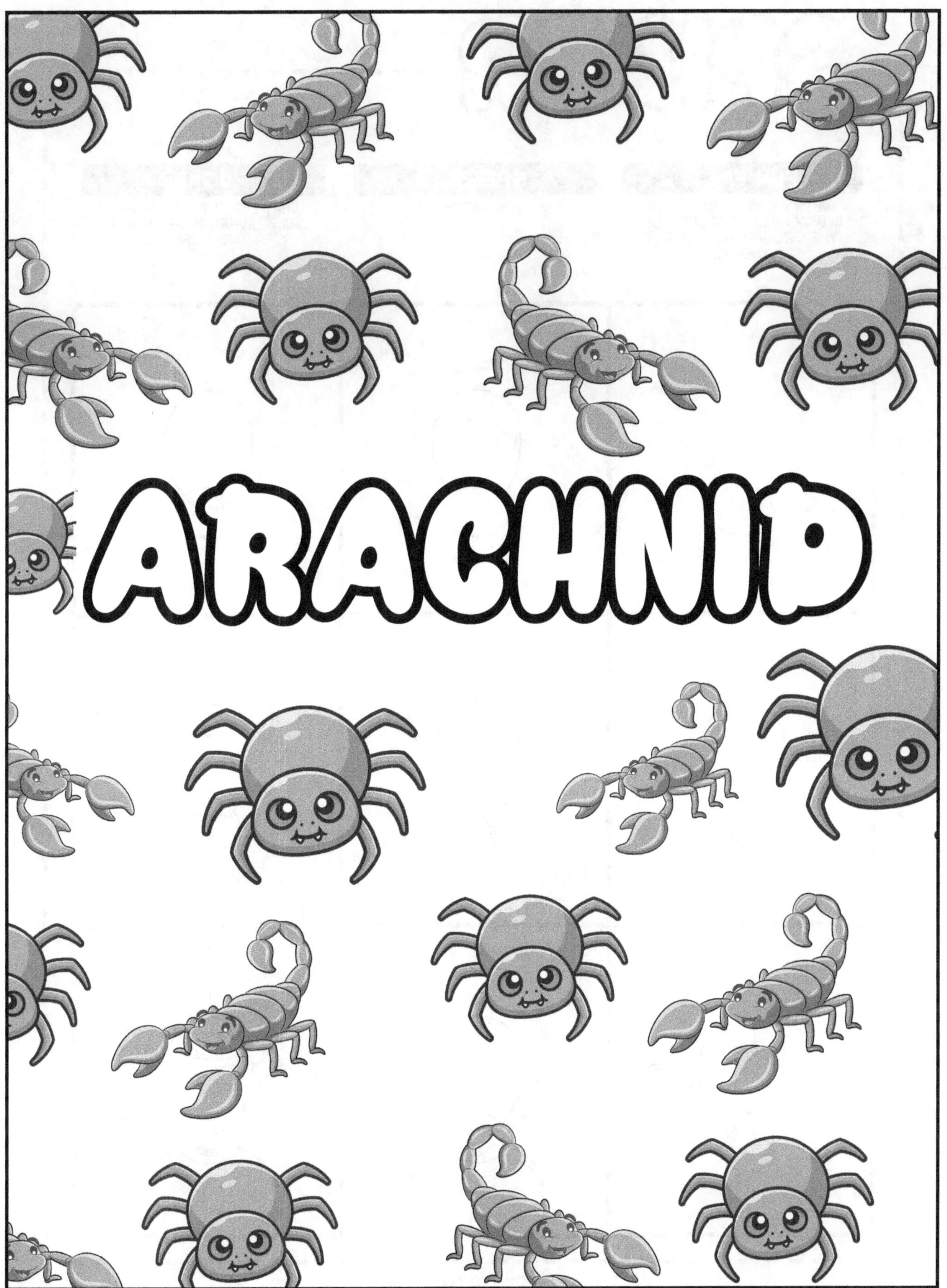

ARACHNID

SPIDER

FUN FACT:
WHEN A SPIDER WALKS, IT ALWAYS HAS FOUR LEGS ON THE GROUND, AND FOUR IN THE AIR.

SPECIES:
45000+

JOKE:
WHAT DID THE SPIDER WANT TO BE WHEN IT GROWS UP? A WEB DESIGNER.

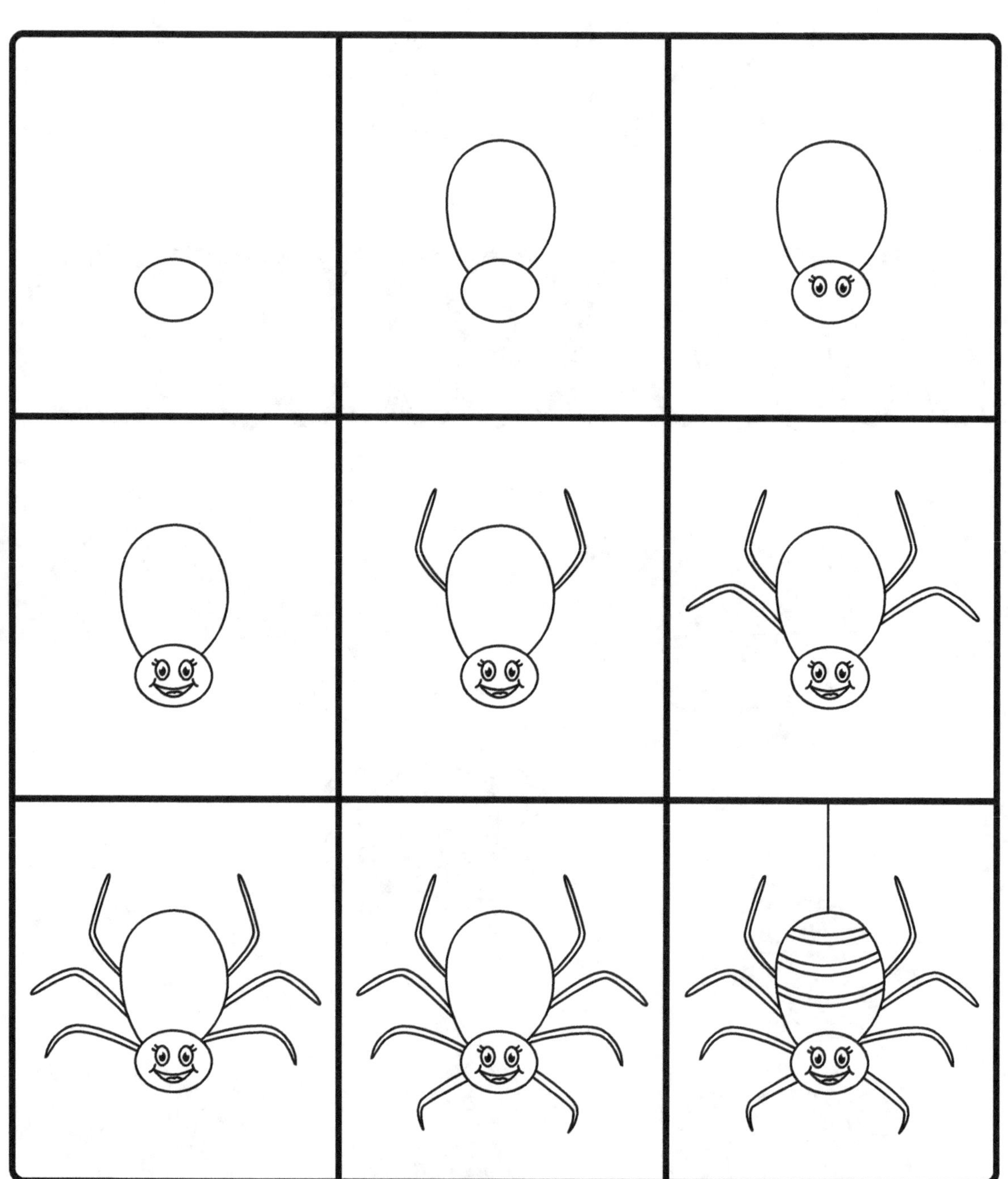

SCORPION

FUN FACT:
SCORPIONS GLOW IN THE DARK!

SPECIES:
2000+

JOKE:
WHY DO SCORPIONS STING?
BECAUSE THEY DON'T KNOW
HOW TO BITE.

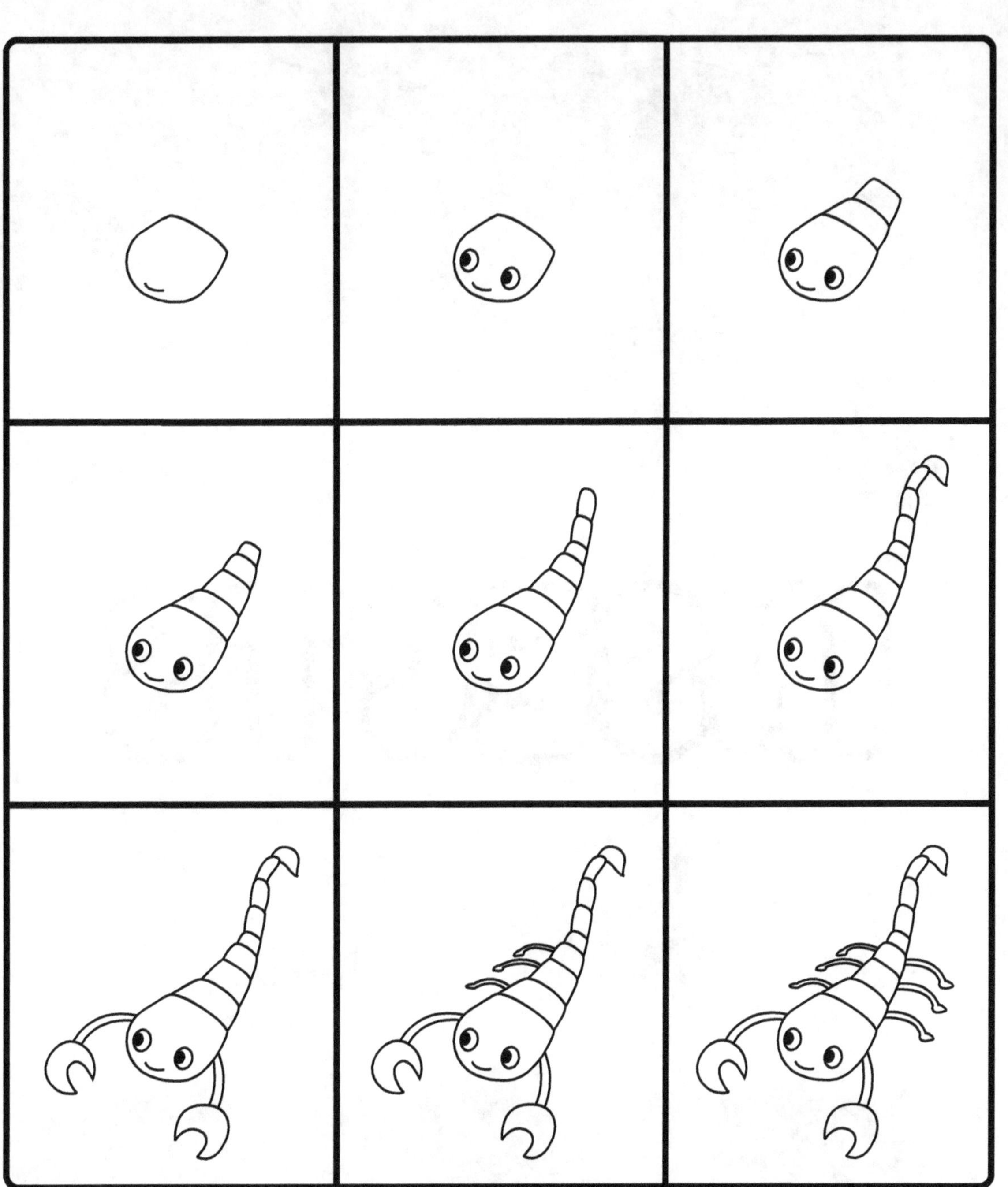

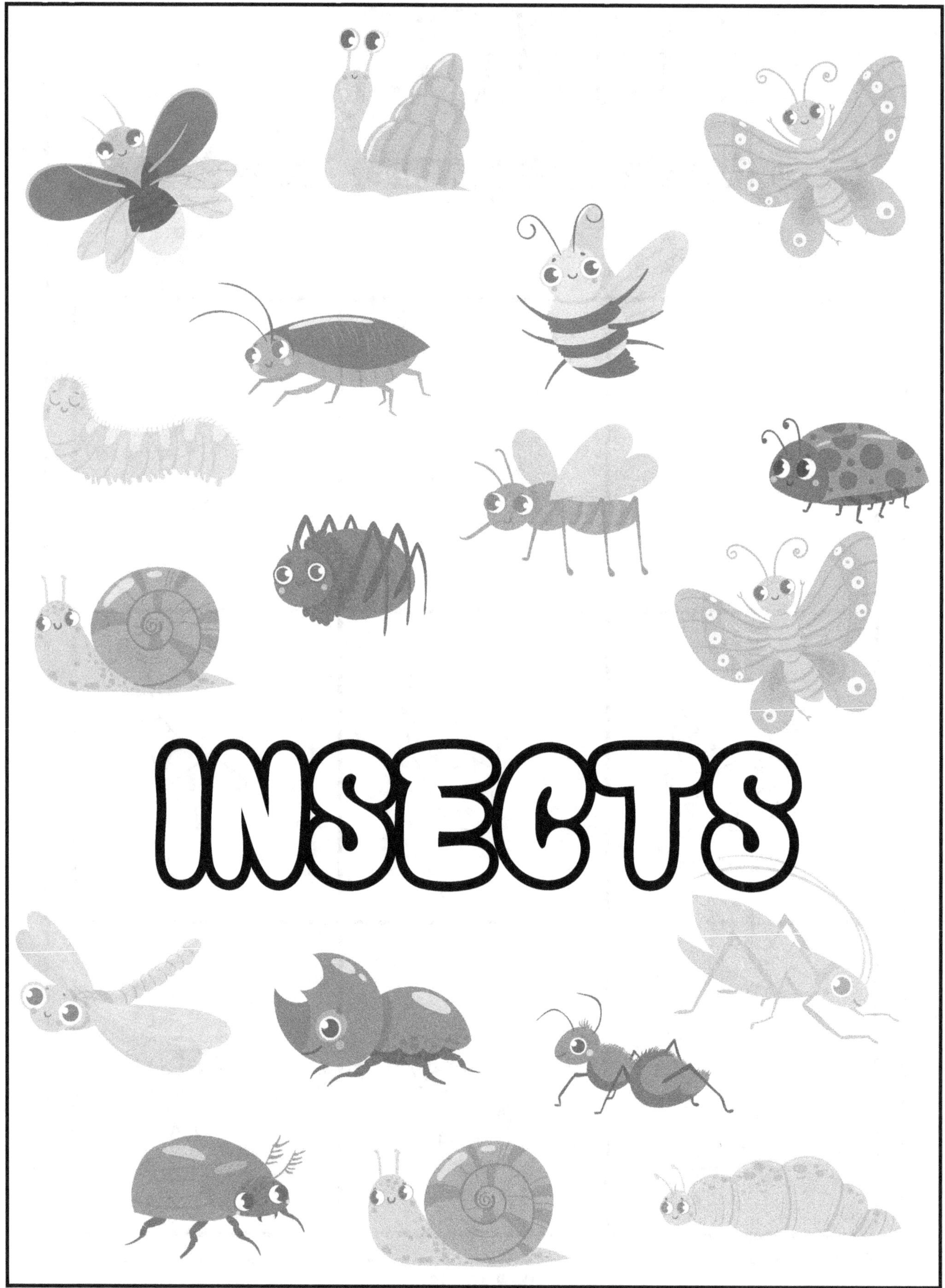

INSECTS

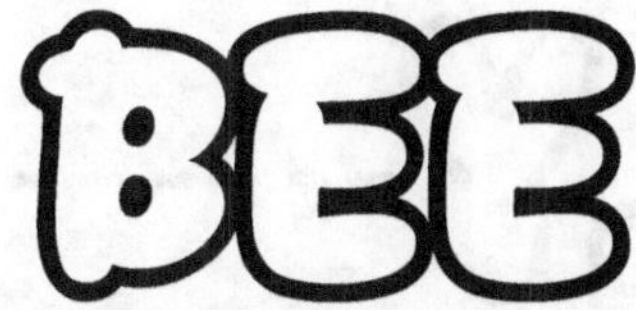

BEE

FUN FACT:
BEES (HONEYBEES) TALK TO
EACH OTHER BY DANCING!

SPECIES:
20,000+

JOKE:
WHAT'S A BEE'S FAVORITE
GAME TO PLAY?
FRIS-BEE.

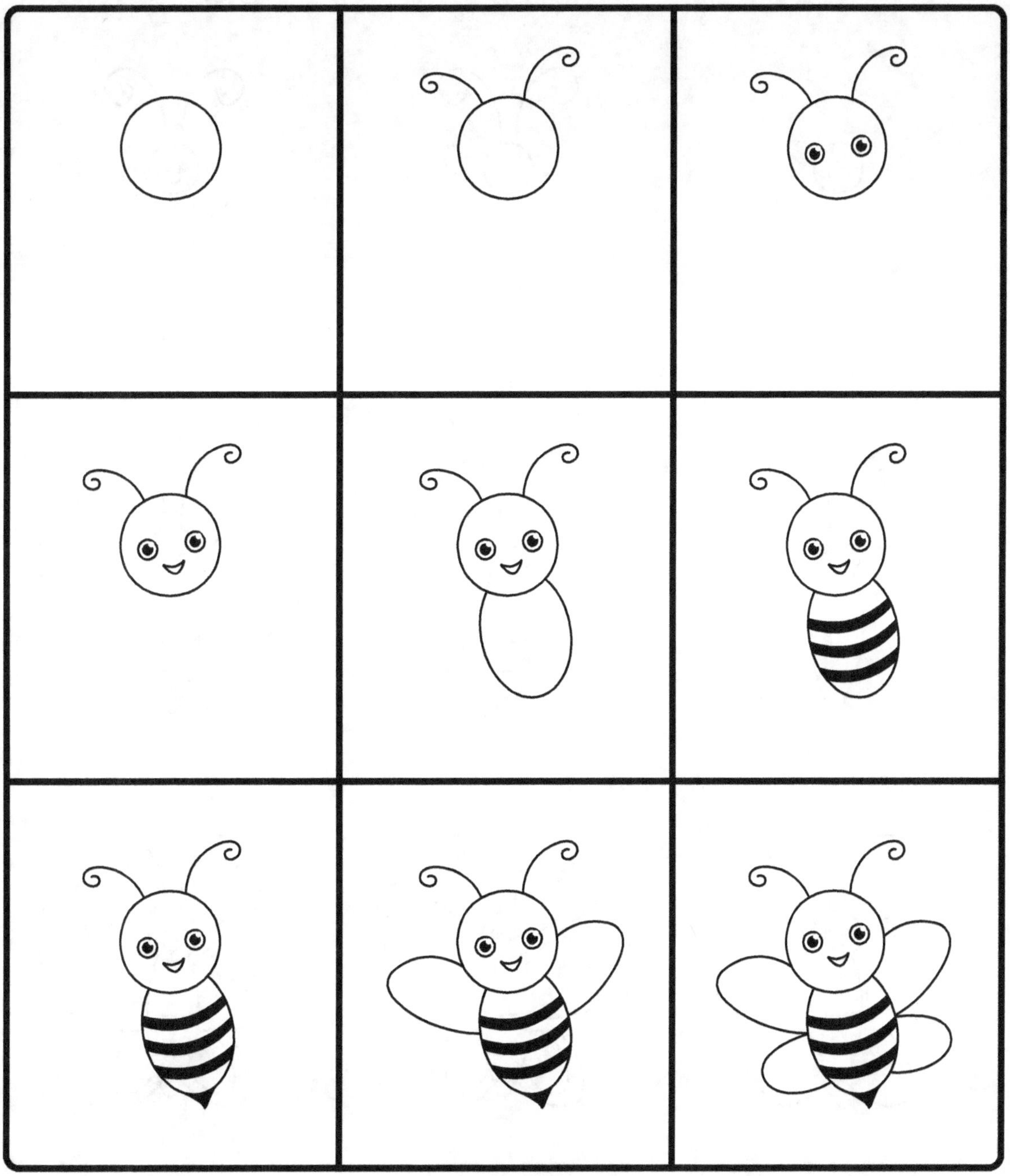

BUTTERFLY

FUN FACT:
THE MONARCH BUTTERFLY'S
BRAIN IS THE SIZE OF A PIN.

SPECIES:
17000+

JOKE:
WHO IS THE MOST ROYAL,
FANCIEST BUTTERFLY OF ALL?
THE MONARCH.

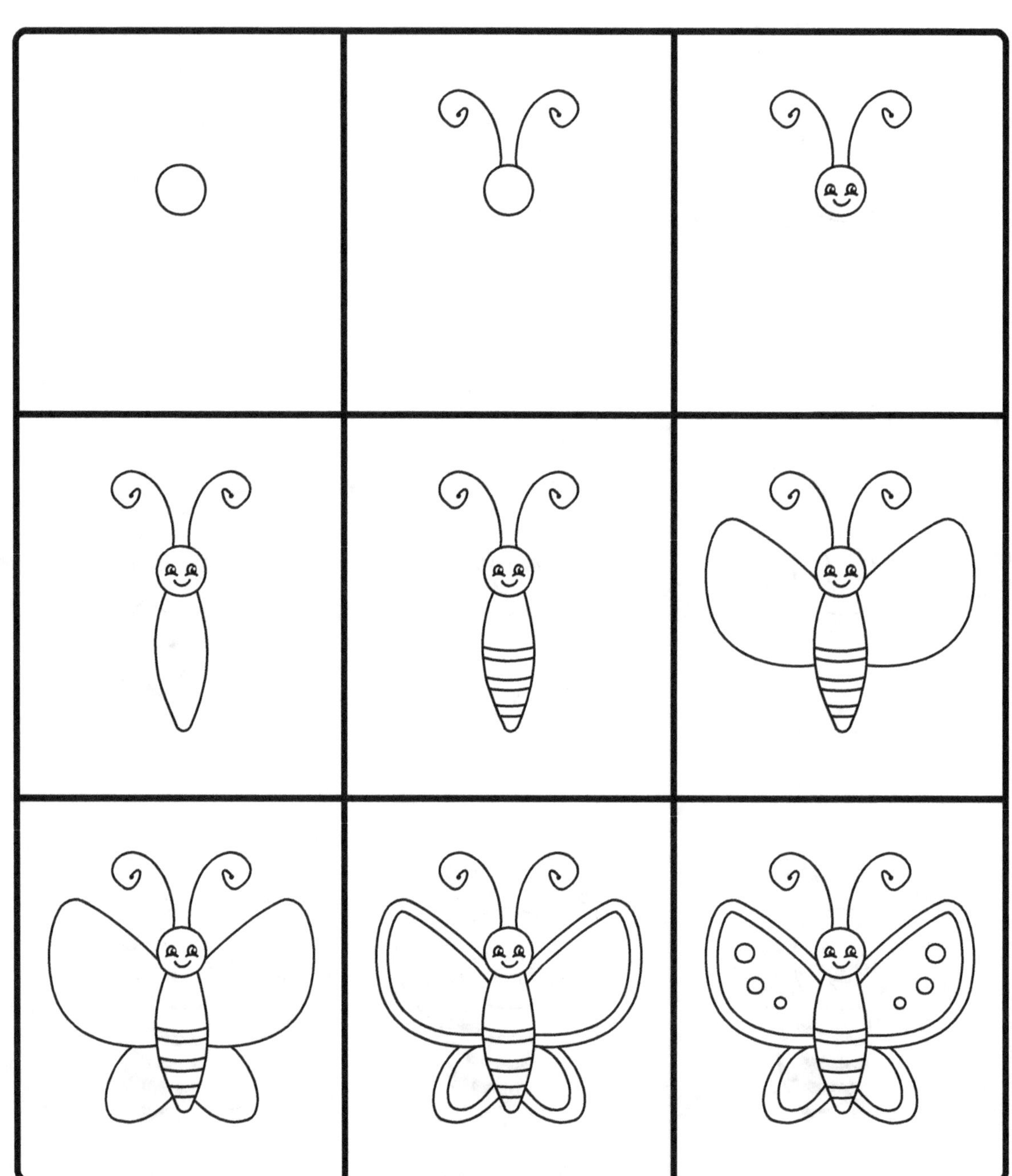

LADYBUG

FUN FACT:
THEY CAN LIVE UP TO THREE
TO FOUR YEARS.

SPECIES:
5000+

JOKE:
WHY DO LADYBUGS HATE TO
PLAY HIDE AND SEEK?
THEY ALWAYS GET SPOTTED.

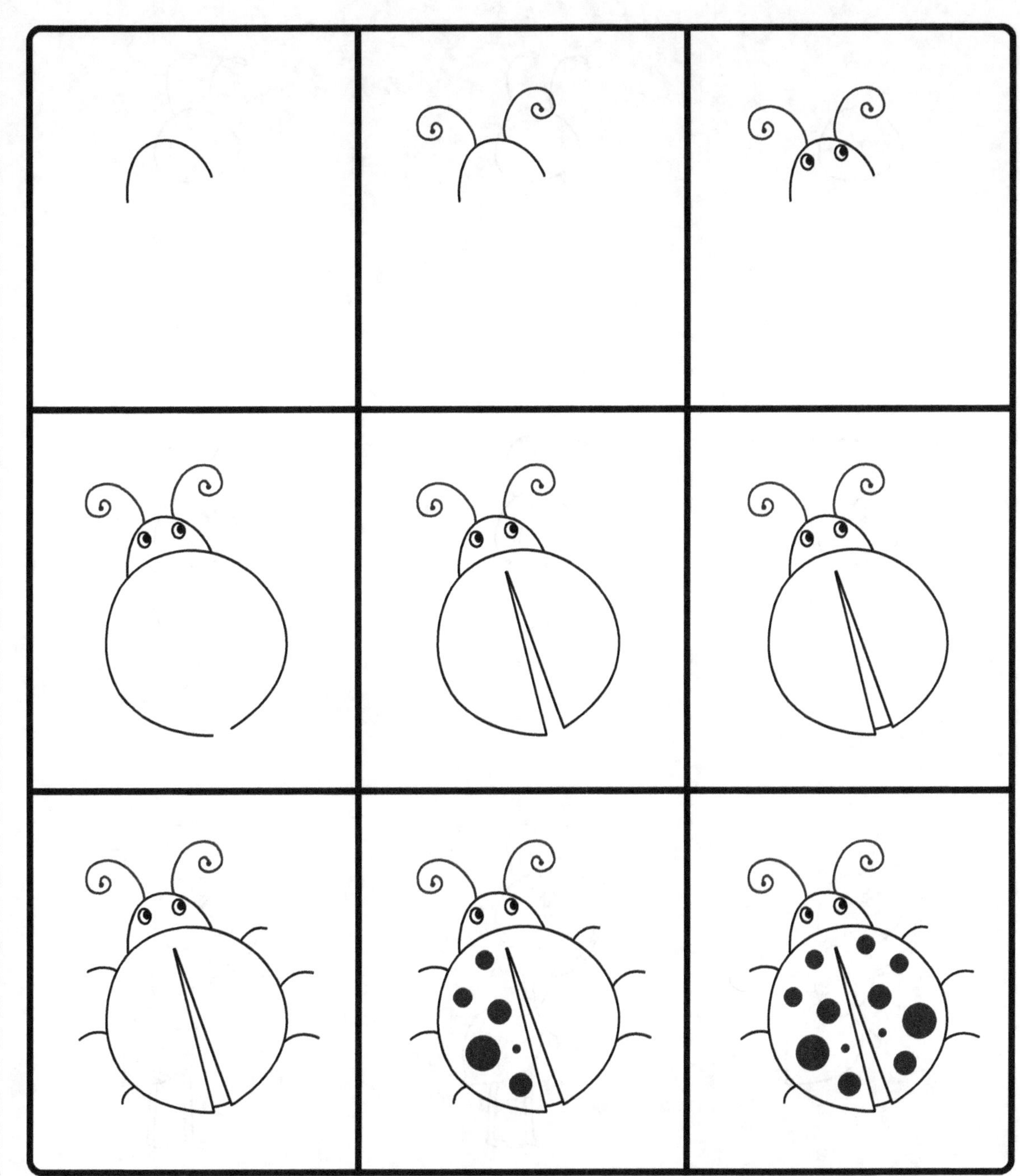

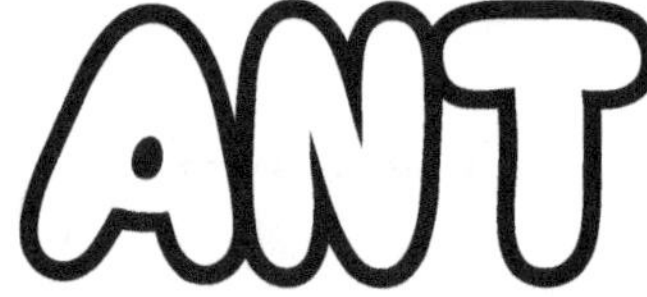

ANT

FUN FACT:
THEY ARE SUPER STRONG AND CAN CARRY UP TO 50 TIMES THEIR BODY WEIGHT.

SPECIES:
10,000+

JOKE:
WHAT DID THE AUNT SAY TO THE ANT?
AUNT YOU A NICE ANT!

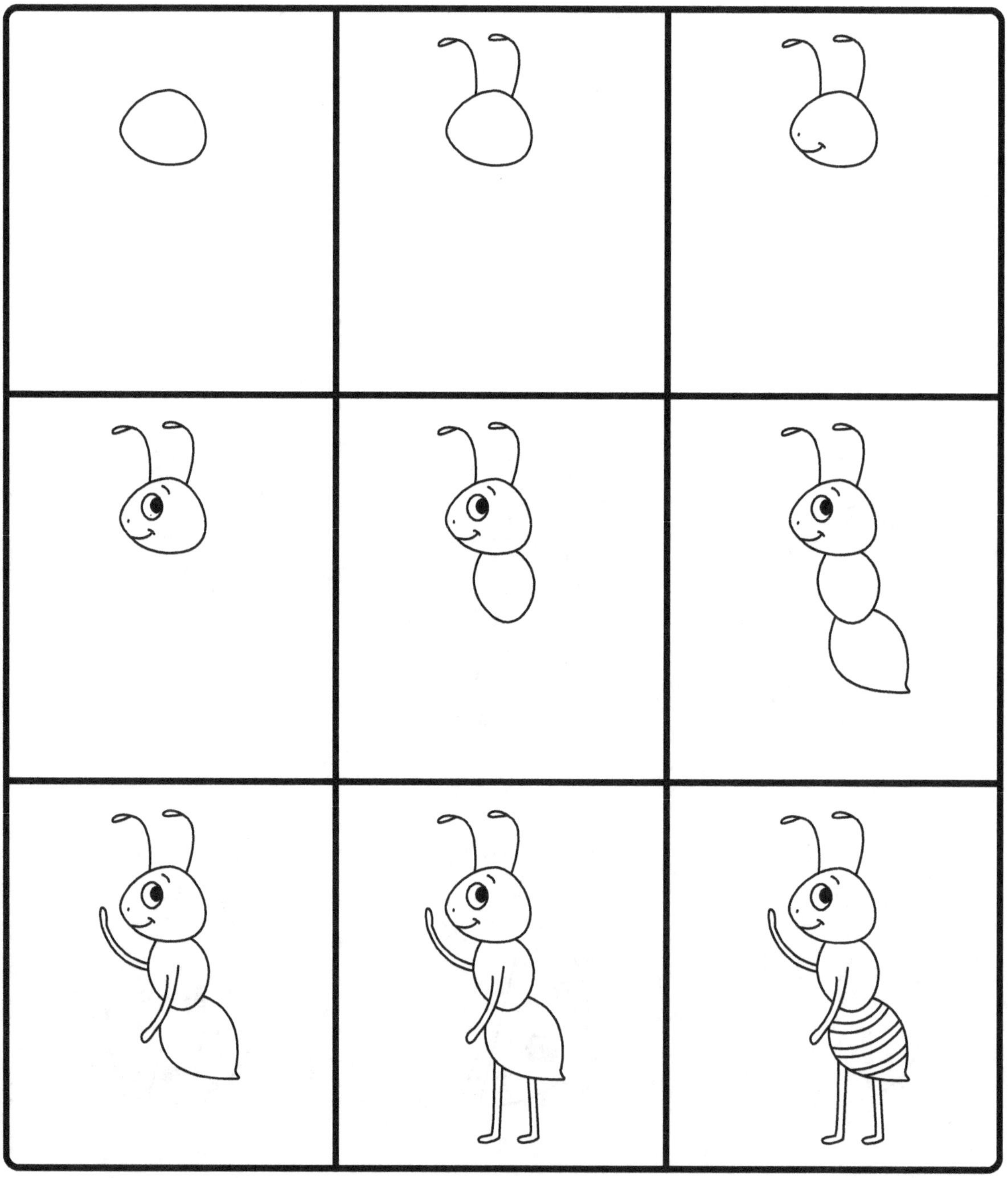

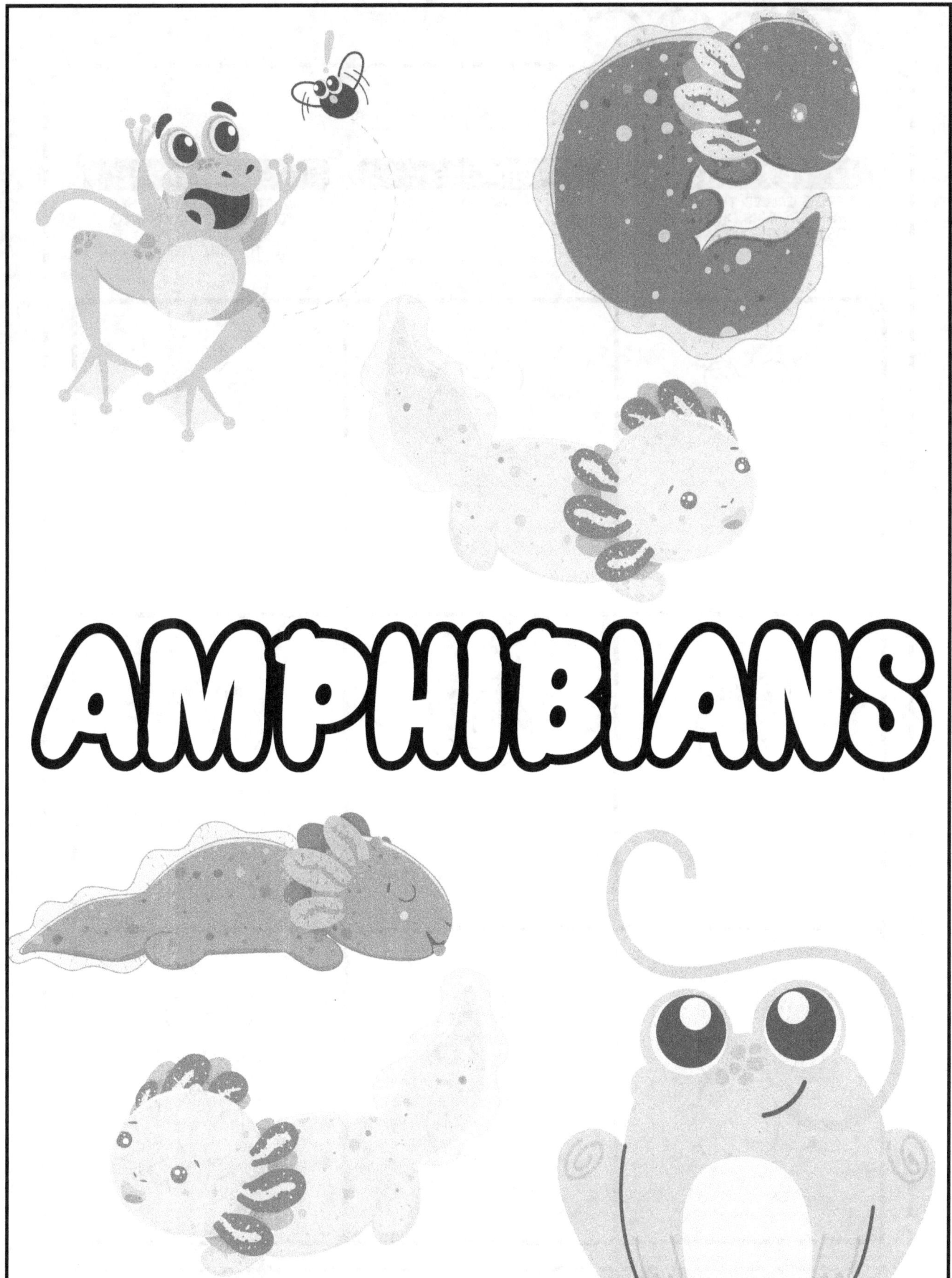

AMPHIBIANS

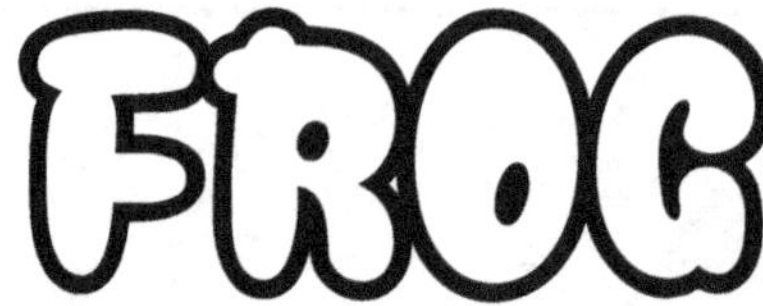

FROG

FUN FACT:
A FROG CALLED THE 'POISON DART FROG' IS ONE OF THE MOST POISONOUS ANIMALS IN THE WORLD.

SPECIES:
6000+

JOKE:
WHAT DO YOU GET WHEN TWO FROGS CRASH INTO EACH OTHER?
TWO TONGUE-TIED FROGS.

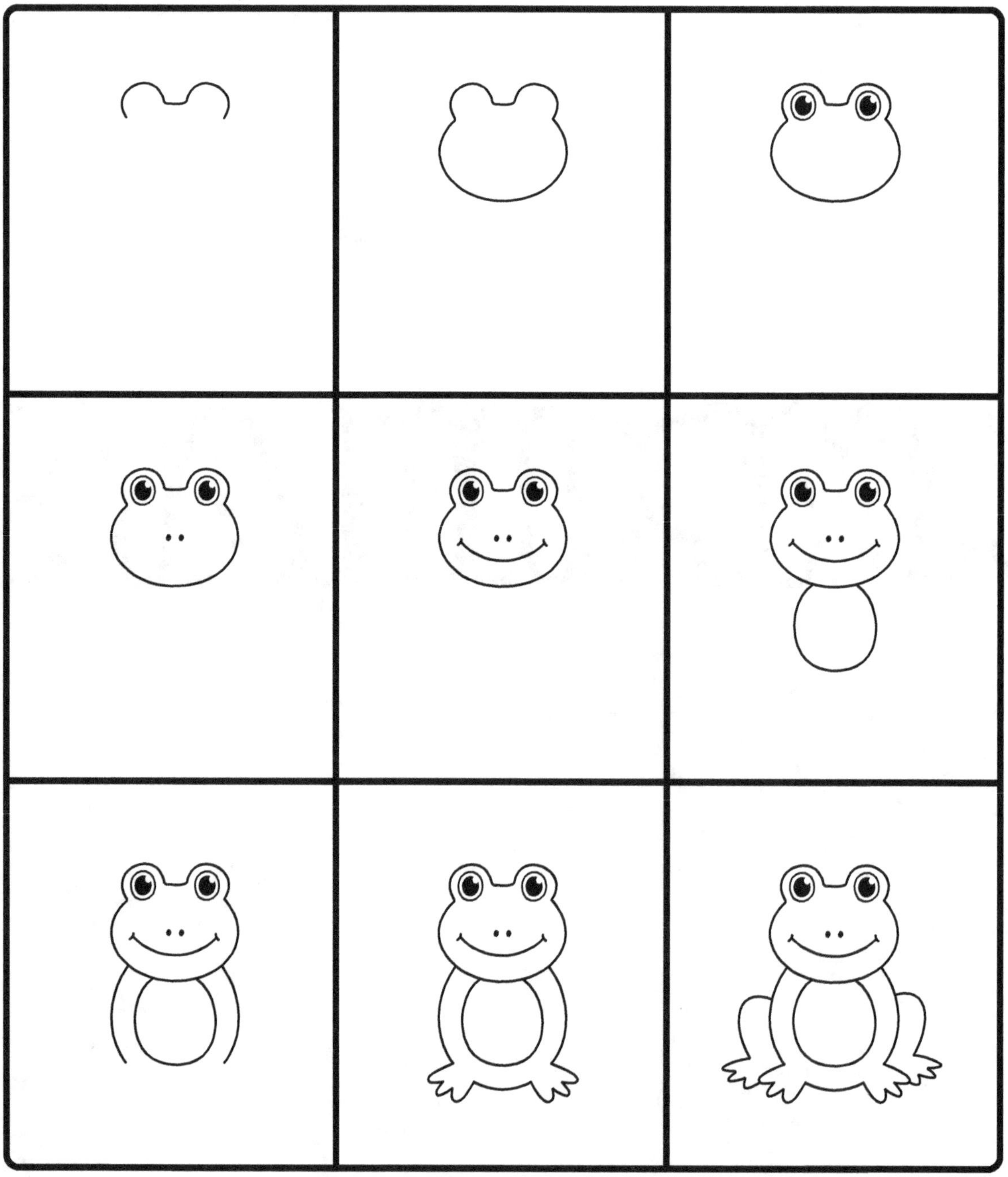

SALAMANDER

FUN FACT:
THEY HIBERNATE WHEN IT'S COLD!

SPECIES:
655

JOKE:
WHY ARE SALAMANDERS SO SMART?
THEY ASK AXOLOTL QUESTIONS.

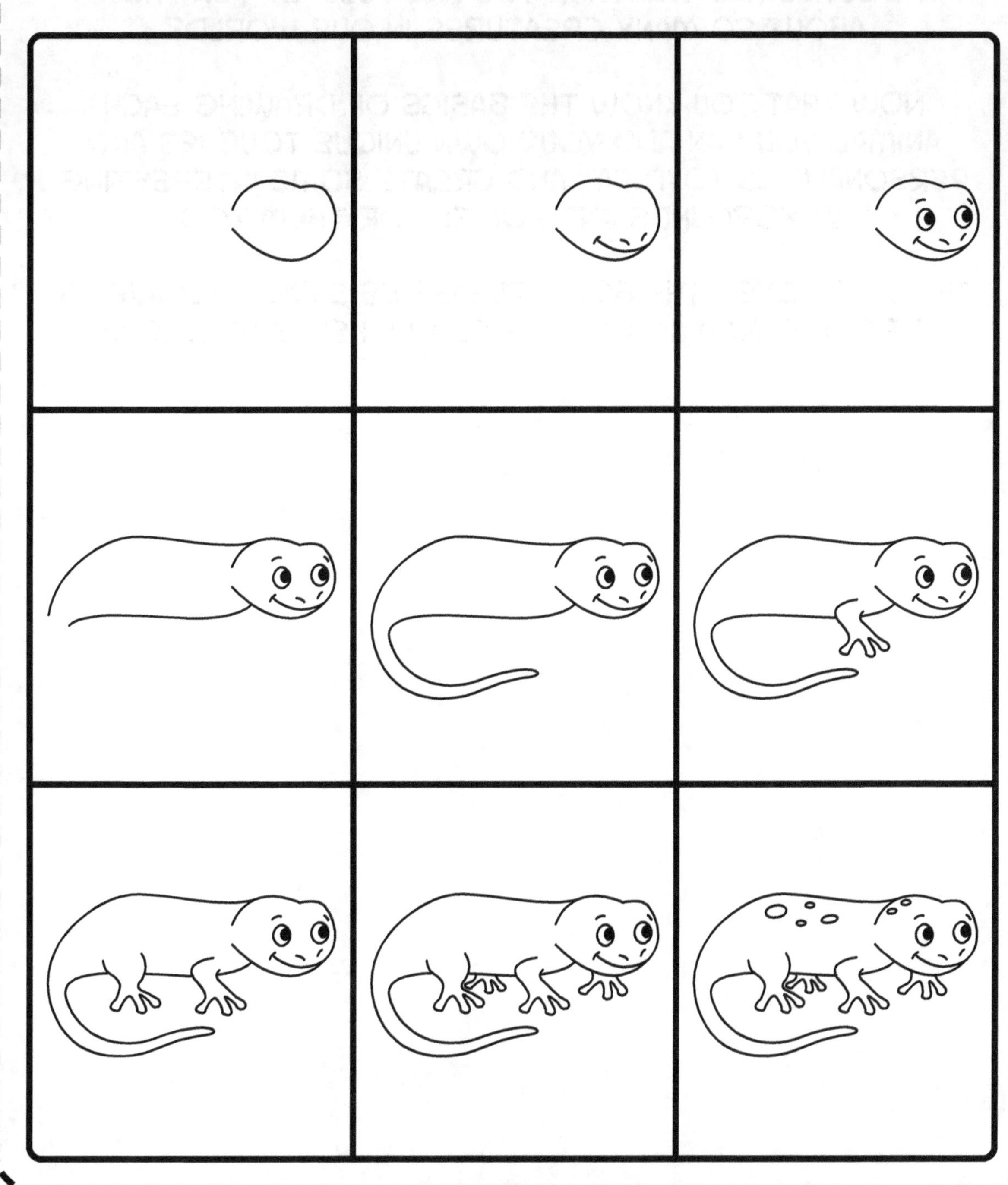

CONCLUSION

SO HOW DID YOU GO DRAWING THESE CUTIE CREATURES? WERE SOME ANIMALS TRICKIER THAN OTHERS? OR SOME MORE FUN TO DRAW? I WONDER IF YOUR FRIENDS LIKED THE JOKES AND WHETHER YOU ARE FULL OF FUN FACTS ABOUT SO MANY CREATURES IN OUR WORLD?

NOW THAT YOU KNOW THE BASICS OF DRAWING EACH ANIMAL, YOU CAN ADD YOUR OWN UNIQUE TOUCHES AND PERSONALITIES TO THEM, AND CREATE SOME INTERESTING BACKGROUNDS AND HOMES FOR THEM TOO.

IF YOU ENJOYED THE BOOK, PLEASE BE SURE TO LEAVE US A REVIEW ON AMAZON AS IT REALLY HELPS US GROW!

www.ingramcontent.com/pod-product-compliance
Lightning Source LLC
Chambersburg PA
CBHW080332030726
47593CB00010B/2981